THE HEM OF HIS GARMENT

Touching the Power in God's Word

Restoration Foundation

Understanding the Jewish roots of our faith is a golden key that unlocks the treasures of Holy Scripture and enriches our Christian lives. This fundamental concept is the focus of Restoration Foundation, an international, transdenominational, multicultural publishing and educational resource to the body of Christ.

Restoration Foundation features a network of scholars, church leaders, and laypersons who share the vision for restoring the Hebrew foundations of Christian faith and returning the church to a biblical relationship of loving support for the international Jewish community and the nation of Israel.

We are pleased to make available to all denominations and fellowships the teaching of the gifted scholars and Christian leaders in our network. Conferences, seminars, and other instructional forums are available on a wide range of topics that can be tailored to each individual setting. These concepts are taught throughout the world in our Restoration Foundation International Institutes.

We publish *Restore!* magazine, a high-quality journal featuring theological balance and scholarly documentation, that helps Christians recover their Hebrew heritage while strengthening their faith in Jesus.

Restoration Foundation also publishes and distributes Golden Key Books in order to disseminate teaching about Christianity's Judaic foundations. The Living Emblems Series is a division of Golden Key Books that offers solid instruction on various biblical symbols, artifacts, and practices that the Jewish people and the church have used to illustrate biblical truths in remembrance of God's mighty acts of history. Living Emblems also makes these items of Judaica available for purchase.

The ministry of Restoration Foundation is made possible by our many partners around the world who share in our Golden Key Partnership program. We invite you to join us in sharing the satisfaction of knowing that you are a partner in an organization that is making a difference in the world by restoring Christians to their biblical Hebrew heritage, by eradicating Judaeophobia and anti-Semitism, by supporting Israel and the international Jewish community, and by encouraging collaborative efforts among those who share this vision.

For information about Restoration Foundation, *Restore!* magazine, Golden Key Books, Living Emblems, and Golden Key Partnerships, contact us at the address below.

Restoration Foundation
P. O. Box 421218
Atlanta, Georgia 30342, U.S.A.
www.RestorationFoundation.org

THE HEM OF HIS GARMENT

Touching the Power in God's Word

By John D. Garr, Ph.D.

GOLDEN KEY BOOKS
Living Emblems Series
Restoration Foundation
P. O. Box 421218
Atlanta, Georgia 30342, U.S.A.

Cover Art by Rachel Unruh, Independence, KS,
and Pam Staley, Foley, MO.

*To my colleagues
around the world who
have enshrouded Pat
and me with loving
concern and have
covered us in the
mantle of their prayers.*

TABLE OF CONTENTS

Foreword

In order to understand the statements Jesus made and the reports of events in his life, we must faithfully employ the grammatico-historical method of scriptural interpretation espoused by the ancient Antiochian School and restored by the sixteenth century church reformers. This linguistic and sociocultural hermeneutic enables us to exegete Scripture tightly within the context of the grammar and the historical and social setting in which it was written, cutting the straight line of interpretation that constitutes "rightly dividing the word of truth."[1]

The lives that Jesus and the apostles lived and the words that they spoke were manifest in the context of their contemporary Jewish culture and of their religion, Second Temple Judaism.[2] The language they spoke was in all probability Hebrew (or at least Western Aramaic, a sister language of Hebrew).[3] Virtually everything they said and wrote was first thought in Hebrew (or Aramaic) and then translated into Greek. If we are to understand the written record of their teachings and of the events of their lives, we must, therefore, study both the *Koinè* Greek of the Apostolic Writings and the Hebrew language and Semitic thought that underlie the Greek text. We must also have a thorough knowledge of the history, culture, and traditions of the first century Jewish people, including their political milieu, their socio-economic circumstances, and their religious practices.

Frequently, very important—even essential—elements necessary for an accurate understanding of what is recorded concerning Jesus' life and ministry are obscured by inadequate translation and/or interpretation of the text itself. We must use as a point of initiation for any New Testament exegesis the fact that Jesus was an observant Jew and that everything he said and did was directed toward his Jewish contemporaries. He himself declared, "I am not sent but unto the lost sheep of the house of Israel."[4] The God whom he addressed as Father was YHWH, the God of Israel; the Bible that he used was the *Tanakh*,[5] the Hebrew Scriptures; the soil which he traversed was Israel, the land of the Jews;[6] and the people who were his family, friends, associates, and even his detractors were Jews. In order to understand the record, therefore, we must look at it through Jewish eyes, or at least we must discard our Greco-Roman and Euro-American eyeglasses and don Hebrew lenses. And, we must be sure that our lenses are positioned in the proper direction so that we are reading out of Scripture what is actually there (exegesis) rather than reading ourselves, our cultures, our philosophies, and our traditions into the record of Scripture (eisegesis).

When we engage ourselves in a search of the Apostolic Writings[7] to discover what the authors said—and not what our presuppositions want them to say—we find a gold mine of enriching truth that transforms our lives into the image of God's dear Son. Every event reported by the evangelists in the Gospels takes on new meaning, because we see the living Jesus not as some extraterrestrial cosmic Christ but as the Son of man, the Jew Jesus living out among his Jewish brethren the paradigm of what it is to be fully human. The *Memra* (*Logos* in Greek), God's eternally preexistent Word, emptied himself of inherent equality with the Father in the *kenosis* of becoming very man. When we see what the essence of God was when he made himself flesh and tabernacled among us, we understand much more about him in his absolute deity. We discover that Jesus truly put a face on the Father[8] by manifesting himself as the "radiance of God's glory and the exact representation of his being."[9]

A knowledge of the Hebrew foundations of Christian faith is vital for all believers in Jesus as Messiah and Lord. By understanding the ancient system of praise, worship, and service through which Jesus and the apostles expressed their devotion to God, we comprehend the motivations for their actions and the basis for their teachings. Christian faith acquires a new depth and meaning when it is understood in the light of the Hebrew matrix from which it emerged. Jesus and the apostles are placed in the context of their Jewish brethren and their religion, Judaism, so that the acts of Jesus and the apostles recorded in the Christian Scriptures from Matthew to Revelation maintain continuity with the acts of God recorded in the Hebrew Scriptures from Genesis to Malachi. Faith in Jesus is then elevated and expanded, given new depth and meaning, not diminished or subsumed into Judaism. The living Messiah is truly seen to be the one who elevated the faith of his heavenly Father and of his fathers according to the flesh by fulfilling it,[10] reforming it,[11] and restoring it to its inherent ideal.[12]

This book explores just one small area of a significant event in the life of Jesus that has for two millennia inspired millions of people with faith in God. It is but one example of the profound wealth of knowledge and inspiration that is often hidden just beneath the surface of Bible translations which do not convey the details or original import of what is reported in Scripture. There are multiplied thousands of other scriptural events and concepts that yet remain to be explored as we continue to dig into the inexhaustible resources of the infinite Word.

I am deeply indebted to some of my closest colleagues and friends for insights that have formed either the basis or the spark of insight upon which many of the ideas outlined and detailed in this book are based. Among them are Dr. Karl D. Coke, president of Redirection Ministries, for his insightful teaching and his writings that have appeared in "Prayer Lessons from Jewish Culture" in *Restore!* magazine and in syllabi for The Timothy Program International; Dr. Douglas A. Wheeler, president of Mended Wings, for his provocative and challenging article, "The Law of the Fringe," that was also published in *Restore!* magazine; Dwight A. Pryor, president of the Center for Judaic-Christian Studies, for his informative audio teaching, "The Mystery of Jesus' Prayer Shawl"; David Bivin, editor of the *Jerusalem Perspective* for his pioneering exposition, "The Hem of His Garment," that appeared in that journal; and Dr. Charles Bryant-Abraham for his masterful theological and linguistic suggestions and help with the manuscript; and to Judy Grehan and Sandy Clark for their careful and constructive reading of the manuscript.

I believe that as you read these pages you will be

challenged to draw nearer to the living Jesus, to walk humbly with him in faith, and to come to the full knowledge of the Son of God.[13] This is the immediate and lasting benefit of understanding the Jewish roots of our Christian faith: we find a foundation of historical and theological truth that anchors our confidence in God's completed work in Christ and sets us on the road to walking with him in maturity and completeness. Understanding the Hebrew foundations of Christian faith is, indeed, a golden key that unlocks the treasures of Holy Scripture.

It is my hope that as you share in this wealth of understanding you will be challenged to "search the Scriptures" to discover for yourself these and untold numbers of additional golden nuggets of truth that will enrich your life. We recognize both the Hebrew Scriptures and the Apostolic Writings as the "God-breathed" Word of God[14] when we fully realize that they are inexhaustible and that the mercies and truths of God which are contained therein are "new every morning."[15]

John D. Garr, Ph.D.
Passover, 1999

---

[1] 2 Timothy 2:15. The Greek word for "rightly dividing" is ὀρθοτομέω (*orthotomeo*) which means to "cut a straight line."

[2] By the first century of the common era "Biblical Judaism" had undergone development that began with Ezra and the "Men of the Great Assembly" and continued through the Tannaim, including the schools of Hillel and Shammai. In many ways, Jesus and the apostles sought to reform Second Temple Judaism by restoring it to biblical foundations, perhaps even encouraging a return to biblical Judaism.

[3] Historically, conventional scholarship has agreed that Western Aramaic was the predominant language of Judaea at the time of Jesus; however, some more recent scholars have suggested that since personal and business documents found at Qumran among the Dead Sea Scrolls were written in Hebrew, Mishnaic Hebrew could still have been commonly understood and spoken in Judaea. Since Jesus and the apostles were focused on religious issues, they could well have taken the

tradition of synagogal liturgical use of Hebrew (translated contemporaneously into other languages) as their guide, thinking and teaching in Hebrew. This would explain the insistence of certain of the Apostolic Fathers that Matthew's Gospel was first written in Hebrew.

[4] Matthew 15:24b.

[5] The word *Tanakh* is actually *TaNaKh*, an acronym for *Torah* (the Pentateuch), *Nevi'im* (Prophets), and *Ketuvim* (Writings–historical and poetic books). Jesus himself made use of this Jewish tradition of the three divisions of the Hebrew Scriptures (e.g., Luke 24:44).

[6] Jesus did venture into Samaria (John 4:4-9) and Phoenicia (Matthew 15:21).

[7] The term *Apostolic Writings* describes what is most commonly termed *The New Testament*. In reality, the New Testament is not a book, but a covenant introduced by Jesus in fulfillment of Jeremiah 31:33. The books of Matthew through Revelation comprise a record by the apostles (or others under their auspices) of the events that occurred under the New Testament.

[8] John 1:18; 14:9.

[9] Hebrews 1:3, NIV.

[10] Matthew 5:17-19.

[11] Hebrews 9:10.

[12] Matthew 5:21-48.

[13] Ephesians 4:12, 13.

[14] 2 Timothy 3:16-17.

[15] Lamentations 3:23.

Chapter 1

A Healing Touch

"If I may but touch his garment, I shall be made whole!" An exclamation of angst, determination, or faith? We can't be sure. There is no doubt, however, that this statement is the centerpiece of one of the most poignant of all Bible stories, an event that unfolds in what was probably a very ordinary day in the life of Yeshua of Nazareth. The humble, unassuming Galilean peasant had long been sought out by growing throngs of suffering people who desperately needed relief from a virtually unending list of maladies and misfortunes. His compassion for the poor, the infirm, the mentally retarded, the emotionally unstable, and the economically and politically disenfranchised had become legendary. He reached out with an empathy that few had ever seen, and he changed lives with a healing touch that had never been witnessed on planet Earth.

This lowly Nazarene had been born some thirty years earlier under most inauspicious circumstances. While a few enlightened believers understood him to be a virgin's son, none of those among whom he grew up ever saw anything extraordinary about him.[1] Much of the general public, and certainly his detractors, considered him illegitimate, born in a stable, wrapped in swaddling clothes. In keeping with the strong devotion to their Jewish faith, his parents had circumcised him on the eighth day, thereby initiating him into the covenant of Abraham. In compliance with the requirements of *pidyon ha-ben* (the redemption of the firstborn), they had presented him at the temple[2] where the astonishing words of both prophet and prophetess predicted wonderful things for his life that would have far-reaching and profound consequences for Israel and the world.[3] He had been reared inconspicuously by his family in a town southwest of the Sea of Galilee whose only claim to fame was that no good thing came from Nazareth.[4]

Jesus had been precocious, to be sure, debating at the age of twelve (possibly shortly after his *bar mitzvah*) with Israel's greatest rabbis during his family's pilgrimage festival observance. But, for the most part, his life was that of an ordinary Jew, being taught in home, synagogue, and temple in Judaism's great truths. He "grew in wisdom and stature, and in favor with God and men."[5] He was employed in his father's business, that of a builder, soiling his hands and straining his body in the construction industry of his day. When he reached the age of thirty, he set out on an itinerant teaching ministry, announcing the imminent breaking forth of the kingdom of God.[6]

Immediately, those around Jesus recognized him to be a rabbi; this, despite the fact that it is nowhere recorded that he had been a student either of Beth Hillel or Beth Shammai, the era's two leading schools of rabbinic thought. He was unique as a teacher, however, for his hearers attested to the fact that he spoke with an authority that the other rabbis of his time did not manifest.[7] He was a lover of the land of Israel and of the *'Am HaAretz* ("people of the land"), or the common folk. His teaching championed honesty, integrity, and human dignity.

Jesus also possessed an amazing gift for the supernatural. Though other Hebrew holy men of that time had frequently manifested preternatural powers, when Jesus spoke, he did so with unheard-of authority so that people were healed *en masse*, demons were exorcized, even the dead were raised. Because of this, some began to think that perhaps he was Elijah returned in spirit and power to prepare the way for the Messiah. Others considered that he might be Jeremiah or another of the prophets.[8] Since there had been no recognized prophet in Israel for some four centuries, this was a distinct honor in itself.

Then, one day as he inquired of his disciples who they considered him to be, Peter, the most outspoken of his followers, exclaimed, "You are he, the Messiah, Son of the living God."[9] Jesus reiterated the fact that there was nothing about his person that would identify him as such: it was a revelation of the Eternal Father. Though he had consistently referred to himself as "Son of Man," both a term of humility (connoting a "human being") and a Messianic title, and despite the fact that he had ascribed to himself eternal preexistence in his "I AM" statements,[10] Jesus' identity as the divinely Anointed of the Jewish people and the Savior of the world had been largely hidden from both the public and his disciples.

On this day, therefore, as he went his way, teaching and touching the lives of those who came to him, one of those who had heard of his reputation for compassion and of his power to mend broken, diseased bodies and wounded, troubled souls was a woman with

a life-threatening condition. We cannot be certain about
the details of this story, but we can imagine, based on
what is recorded, that her condition was grave. Frail,
emaciated, anemic, she was but a shell of her former
vivacious, ebullient self. Her youthful beauty had dissolved into the haggard look of weakness. Her ashen
face was punctuated by the thin lips and the clenched
jaw of a determination to survive. She was desperate.
"If I can but touch his garment, I shall be made whole,"
she said to herself.

This poor woman had been hemorrhaging for
twelve years, probably with menorrhea, a condition
that rendered her both physically weak and psycho-
logically depressed because her malady made her per-
petually unclean according to the ceremonial laws of
her people and had probably long since been cause for
divorce as "unfit for cohabitation." If she even touched
other people, they contracted *tumiah* ("ritual impu-
rity") and would continue to communicate her "un-
cleanness" to others unless they immersed in a *mikveh*
and waited until evening to be pronounced "clean"
again. How embarrassing! In such desperation, these
words of hope echoed like a chant, rising like a cre-
scendo in her troubled mind: "If I can but touch his
garment, I shall be made whole."

Trying to find a cure for her condition, she had
spent all of her resources on physicians and had only
grown worse, perhaps even the victim of medical mal-
practice or ineptitude. Now, here she was, a poverty-
stricken, emotionally-wrecked, physically-broken waif,
possessing only one faint hope of deliverance from
certain death: "If I can but touch his garment, I shall
be made whole!" she repeated to herself.

So, defying all social convention, she mustered

up the last reserves of her strength and pressed her way through the multitude that was thronging the Rabbi, hanging on his every word, and reacting to his every gesture. How she made her way through the crowd, no one knows, but in her heart of hearts she just knew, "If I can but touch his garment, I shall be made whole!" She didn't need a word; she needed a touch. And, touch him she did. In one desperate lunge, she reached out her bony, near-lifeless hand and brushed against just the hem of Jesus' garment. The fact that she touched just the hem of his garment may be an indication that she was crawling through the thronged, huddled bodies. A miracle happened: immediately her hemorrhaging stopped. She was made whole!

Jesus realized that something had occurred because of the release of power from his own person. When he inquired, "Who touched me?", his disciples replied incredulously, "With this multitude thronging you, how can you ask, 'Who touched me?'" Then she who had been stooped, emaciated, and cowering suddenly stood tall, so tall that she could not hide herself in the crowd, and she confessed to the Rabbi what she had done. Even though he might have been rendered ceremonially unclean by the biblical society's standards (if she had touched his flesh), Jesus affirmed this woman's hopes, saying, "Daughter, thy faith hath made thee whole; go in peace, and be whole of thy plague."

What a wonderful story of extraordinary and powerful emotion! Desperation and faith produced a profound miracle for a simple daughter of Israel. What a wonderful Savior, this Jesus, who had the power to heal just by being touched even when he was unaware of what had happened! "If I can but touch his garment, I shall be made whole!"–words that have inspired faith in the hearts of millions of believers in the Jesus of the Gospels.

 But, there's more to the story!

[1] See Matthew 13:54-57 and Mark 6:1-3.

[2] Luke 2:22-24.

[3] Luke 2:32.

[4] John 1:46.

[5] Luke 2:52, NIV.

[6] Matthew 11:12, the centerpiece of Jesus' proclamation concerning the kingdom should be translated: "The kingdom of God is breaking forth [*like the walls of a sheepfold*], and passionate men press their way into it."

[7] Mark 1:22.

[8] In Second Temple Judaism, the concept of *gilgul ha-nephasot* was a common view, suggesting that the spirit of one prophet could return upon someone else in another era. This concept is alluded to in Luke 1:17 in Gabriel's annunciation to Zacharias and in Matthew 11:14 in Jesus' evaluation of John the Baptizer. This phenomenon is likely interpreted as being the return of the spirit (or the frame of mind or line of thought) that motivated a man of God of one era upon another person in another time. It may well also have implied that God could return that measure of his Holy Spirit which distinctively motivated a prophet in one era upon another person at a subsequent time.

[9] Matthew 16:16 (author's translation).

[10] John 8:58; 11:25; 14:6.

Chapter 2

The Hem of the Garment

The story in Matthew 9 is not just an isolated, one-of-a-kind event in the life of Jesus when a lone woman reached out and touched the hem of his garment to be healed. In Matthew 14:35, 36, this story is reported: "And when the men of [Gennesaret] had knowledge of him, they sent out into all that country round about, and brought unto him all that were diseased; and besought him that they might only touch the hem of his garment: and as many as touched were made perfectly whole." Could it be that touching the hem of Jesus' garment became a common practice, with untold numbers of people–not just one woman or the diseased of one region–healed by such a simple touch? What was it about the "hem of his garment" that was so important that it should become a point of contact for the expression of faith that brought deliverance to all who touched it?

Hidden from the eye of the reader of these stories is an enriching key to understanding what actually occurred on these days of deliverance. Virtually all translations of these passages of Holy Scripture render an incomplete portrayal of the actual object of the desperate woman's determined hand and of the touch of the diseased of Gennesaret. Most Christians imagine

Jesus wearing a sumptuous robe and the woman touching the broad decorative band that was the hem of his robe. After all, as one person was heard to remark, "That's the way he looked in all the photos we have of him!"

Most versions of the Bible tell us that she touched the "hem of his garment"[1] or the "border of his garment"[2] or the "edge of his cloak"[3] or the "fringe of his cloak."[4] None of these translations, however, adequately conveys one important detail of the event. Without this detail, we simply miss the richness of this event and of an entire tradition in biblical history.

The word in the Greek text for "hem" is κράσπεδον (kraspedon), which means "the extremity or prominent part of a thing, edge, skirt, margin; the fringe of a garment; the appendage hanging down from the edge of the mantle or cloak, made of twisted wool; a tassel or tuft." Κράσπεδον (kraspedon) is the Greek word that was used to translate the Hebrew word צִיצִת (tzitzit) in the Septuagint Version of the Hebrew Scriptures. (Scholars in Alexandria in the fourth century B.C.E. rendered this version in order to provide the Scriptures in the lingua franca of the Mediterranean Basin.) What the woman touched, then, was not a broad decorative band at the skirt of Jesus' garment, but the fringe, the twisted woolen tassel hanging from the edge of his mantle or cloak.

Jesus was in every way a very proper, Torah-observant Jew, not a blue-eyed, fair-skinned, brown-haired European Christian as he has so often been portrayed. He wore the clothing traditional to the Jewish people of his day. Contrary to popular Christian tradition, Jesus was not rebelling against the faith of his fathers, the religion of the First Testament. He was a believing, practicing Jew who fully observed the heritage in which he had been trained by his parents. They "did everything according to the law of Moses,"[5] the Scripture tells us. This Jesus was a Jew, and the religion which he observed throughout his lifetime was the faith of his fathers, *Derekh ha-Torah*, "the Way of the Torah." He made no bones about it: "We know what we worship: for salvation is from the Jews," he declared.[6]

Jesus was recognized as being Jewish by the woman at the well of Samaria by his outward appearance. His grooming and his style of dress immediately identified him as a Jew. First, in obedience to the commandments, the edges of his beard and the hair at the sides of his head would not have been cut.[7] Secondly, both the style and design of his clothing were distinctively Jewish. The outer garment that he wore was called in Greek ἱμάτιον (*himation*) or in Latin *pallium*, meaning a rectangular, four-cornered cloak, mantle, or tunic. This differed from the Roman *toga*, which was semicircular in design. In He-

Tallit **worn by Jewish men**

brew, this garment was first termed *adderet* or *me'il*. Later it came to be called טַלִּית (*tallit*). Some have suggested that the Hebrew word *tallit* is an adaptation of the Greek στολή (*stole*),[8] from which we get the name of the vestment that is worn by liturgists in sacramental churches.

Additionally, in order to fulfill the law day by day Jesus would also have also worn *tefillin*, the two leather pouches (boxes) in which the Word of God was to be bound to the arm and forehead according to Exodus 13:9, 16 and Deuteronomy 6:6-8; 11:18. When *tefillin* are mentioned in most versions of the New Testament, they are

Tefillin **worn by Jewish men**

called phylacteries, a translation of the Greek word meaning "a safeguard" (implying an amulet or talisman, a pagan superstition designed to ward off evil spirits). While some Jews in Bible times may well have been superstitious, considering *tefillin* as charms to protect themselves from evil, the wearing of *tefillin* was a fully biblical practice designed by God himself and practiced by Jewish men as a material reminder that they were to bind God's Word on their foreheads and on their hands (arms) and to write his Word in their minds and hearts.

We can be certain that Jesus observed each of these features of grooming and dress because they were requirements of the Torah (law), the violation of which was sin (cf. 1 John 3:4: ". . . sin is the transgression of the law."). Because Jesus was born "under the law,"[9] sinlessness for him meant complete Torah observance, including the *mitzvot* governing dress and grooming. Since the record of Scripture emphatically affirms the fact that Jesus was without sin,[10] we must draw the conclusion that he was fully observant of the written law of God in its most minute detail. His contentions with his fellow Jews over legalisms and hypocrisy, including those denunciations of "broad" *tefillin* (phylacteries) and "long" *tzitzit*, were focused entirely on interpretations of Torah and applications of oral tradition, not on the authority of the *Tanakh*, the written Word of God. Jesus, himself, testified un-

How *Tefillin* are bound to the arm and forehead

equivocally: ". . .I have kept my Father's commandments."[11] He was a Torah-observant Jew; therefore, he was not negligent in obeying his Father's commandments regarding dress and grooming.

When the woman and the people of Genessaret touched the *tzitzit* on Jesus' *tallit,* they were operating under a Hebraic tradition of respect for God and his Word. What they did was not profoundly unusual in first century Israelite society. For the common people, their sages were living examples of separation unto God's Word; therefore, their clothing and other items associated with them had special significance, even sacredness. It was an honor to touch a rabbi's clothing. Being healed by the touch of a prophet, sage, or miracle

worker also occurred not infrequently in Israel. Jesus
the Jew was merely continuing the tradition of many
before and during his time, of reaching out to the op-
pressed with a hand of mercy. The woman and the
citizens of Gennesaret were operating in that tradition
when they reached out to grasp the *tzitzit* that Rabbi
Jesus wore. They were laying hold on the visible symbol of the totality of the Torah and by doing so were
touching in a spiritual dimension the God of the universe.

Originally, the word *tallit* (pl. *tallitot*) meant
"gown" or "cloak" and referred to the rectangular, four-
cornered, blanket-like mantle worn by men in ancient
times (quite similar to the *poncho* of Latin American
culture). It was made either of wool or of linen[12] and
probably resembled an *'abbayah* ("blanket"), the ori-
ental robe still worn by the Bedouin Arabs for protection against the weather.[13] A *tallit* of finer quality
resembling the Roman *pallium* was worn by the
wealthy and by distinguished rabbis.[14]

This may have been the *tallit* that was also described by the Hebrew word סָדִין (*sadiyn*) (Greek:
σινδον, *sindon*), a rectangular piece of fine linen worn
as an outer garment during the day or as the sole garment at night. These were the fine linen garments that
the woman of valor was praised by her husband for
making. This passage in Proverbs 31 is said to have
originated in Abraham's praise for Sarah and as such
may be an indication of an even more ancient origin
for the *tallit* or at least of its precursor, the *sadiyn*.

This expensive fine linen garment was also used
to cover the bodies of the dead. This may well further
elucidate on the fact that in his entombment, Jesus
was wrapped in fine linen. He was likely covered by

Joseph of Arimathea with a fine linen *sadiyn* or *tallit*, so that both in life and in death, Jesus was physically covered with the outward symbol of the authority of God's Word, the Torah.

Initially, the *tallit* was not an extra vestment (as in later times). It was merely the outer four-cornered garment to which the *tzitziot* were appended.[15] According to Jewish tradition this garment had to be a hand's breadth shorter in length than the garment under it.[16] The inner garment was a tunic (called *haluk* in Hebrew) and could be worn in the home or when one was engaged in physical activity where the outer robe would be too cumbersome. The outer garment, the *tallit* (*himation, pallium*), was essential for public occasions, for despite the fact that the inner robe extended to just above the ankles, it would have been considered immodest in Jewish society for one to appear in public without the *tallit*. If necessary, one could appear in public only in a *tallit*, but not solely in a *haluk*.[17] Recognizing the fact that two robes were worn in Jesus' time helps us to understand his statement in Matthew 5:40 (NIV): "If someone wants to sue you and take your tunic [*haluk*, tunic], let him have thy cloak [*tallit*, *himation*, *pallium*] as well." It was better in Jesus' mind for one to appear immodest than to be a contentious person.[18]

After the *Galut* (Hebrew for "exile") or *Diaspora* (Greek for "dispersion") of the Jews in the Babylonian captivity, the Jewish people came to adopt the fashions of their Gentile neighbors. This was particularly true of those who chose to remain outside Israel following the exile. (Of the two million who were carried into captivity, 96% remained in Babylon after the edict of Cyrus permitted the return to Jerusalem and the rebuilding of the Temple.)   Such conformity to popular styles of dress was not unusual, however, for the Jews had always assimilated garment designs from their neighbors, simply adapting *tzitzit* to the fashions of the day. After the time of Alexander the Great, Greek fashions became the social norm throughout the Seleucid Empire and Greater Persia.

As time progressed, many of the Jewish people found themselves wearing clothing that had no distinctive corners to which they could attach fringes; therefore, the traditional *tallit* gradually faded into disuse. Anxious to maintain fulfillment of the commandment, however, the Jews decided to retain the robe, not as a main garment, but as a shawl or surplice worn as a religious garment: the prayer shawl. The name *tallit* was maintained through the centuries for this liturgical garment. By wearing this surplice during the day, the Jewish people could continue to wear the *tzitzit* (fringes), which were essential to the fulfillment of the commandment. Again, as fashion changed and the wearing of a fringed surplice became an incongruity, the Jewish people came to wear the *tallit* only for prayer, in both home and synagogue.[19] Until well after the destruction of the Temple and the Roman occupation, the Jews in Israel continued to wear the *tallit* as a simple outer garment with *tzitziyot* attached in the four corners. The transition from *tallit* and *tzitzit* that were worn throughout the day to *tallit* as a praying shawl was not complete even for Jews in the Diaspora until centuries later. The modern "prayer shawl" is much more recent, dating only to the time of Medieval Europe.

Obviously, this was not the original intent of the *mitzvah*, for the *tzitzit* was to remind the Jews of the commandments at all times, requiring that they be worn at all times. At an early period, the answer for many Jews was to devise a "*tallit katan,*" a miniature *tallit* complete with fringes that could be worn under the outer garments. This garment, also called "*arba kanfot*" (four corners), is a rectangular piece of cloth made of linen, silk, or wool with an aperture in the center through which the head can pass. It has the four essential corners to which the *tzitziyot* are attached. Orthodox men wear the *tallit katan* from the age of three[20] throughout their lives. This is in keeping with Rashi's observation that "it is more important to be garbed in *tzitzit* in the

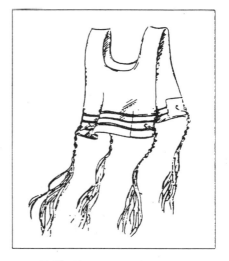

Tallit Katan worn by many Jewish men

hours other than the time of prayer in order that one remember at all times, and not go astray and commit a sin; for at the time of prayer one does not sin."[21] Even in death, a Jewish man is wrapped in his *tallit* with one of the *tzitziyot* cut or removed (which renders it *pasul*, or invalid).

Rudolph Brasch made this observation concerning the historical transition in manifestation of the *tallit* among the Jews: "A positive symbol of a life dedicated to God fell in stature to the role of a praying-shawl. The tsitsit, once proudly and visibly worn as a signpost to pure living, were relegated to form part of an undergarment, often deteriorating in people's minds from an ethical symbol to a superstitious talisman. Yet, in spite of such temporal devaluation and displacement, the tallit itself always preserved its potent symbolism . . . No deterioration could detract from its mission. Today, when the Jew puts on his tallit, numerous thoughtful and incisive messages stir and challenge his mind."[22]

It has been suggested that the Jewish people could avoid the entire *mitzvah* of *tzitzit* by simply not wearing a garment with four corners, for the *tzitzit* is required to be appended only to the corners of such a garment. As styles of clothing changed over the centuries, Jews could perhaps have discontinued this practice altogether; however, the commandments regarding the wearing of *tzitzit* required the Jews to make for themselves *tzitzit* "throughout their generations," which implied that even in generations when Israelites no longer were accustomed to wearing four-cornered garments, they should still make four-cornered garments and attach *tzitziyot* to them, thereby fulfilling the Numbers 15:38 commandment "throughout the generations to come" (NIV).

Due to the gradual change in the style and manner of fulfilling the commandment of *tzitzit*, we cannot know the exact state of the *tallit* in Jesus day with absolute certainty. We can be sure, however, that it was not the prayer shawl of modern times. Misunderstanding this historical fact has given rise to the *New International Version's* translation of Matthew 23:5: "They make . . . the tassels of their prayer shawls [κράσπεδον . . . ἱμάτιον (*kraspedon. . .himation*)] long." In the days of Jesus, the *tallit* had not yet become the modern praying surplice, used at the time of morning prayer. It was still an outer garment worn throughout the day when one was in public. Incidentally, it is quite ironic that, while the *New International Version* translates the Greek words κράσπεδον . . .ἱμάτιον (*kraspedon. . .himation*) as "tassels of their prayer shawls" when referring to Jews and hypocrisy in Matthew 23:5, it translates precisely the same phrase (κράσπεδον . . .ἱμάτιον) as "the hem of his garment" when referring to Jesus and divine healing in Matthew 9:20. Is this merely coincidental, the preservation of a tradition, or is it an effort to conceal Jesus' identity as an ordinary Jew living among and interacting with his Jewish brethren?

What we do know for certain is that since he was a faithful, Torah-observant Jew, Jesus fulfilled God's commandment to wrap himself in the *tzitzit*. To the general public both from Israel and from the nations round about, he could immediately be recognized as a Jew by the flowing tassels that were attached to his *tallit*. He, too, like all observant Jewish males of his day, was a walking reminder that God's people were to remember all his commandments and do them.

---

[1] Matthew 9:20.
[2] Luke 8:44.
[3] Matthew 9:20, NIV.
[4] Matthew 9:20, NRV.
[5] Luke 2:39.
[6] John 4:22.
[7] Leviticus 19:27: "Ye shall not round the corners of your heads, neither shalt thou mar the corners of thy beard."
[8] W.O.E. Oesterly. *The Religion and Worship of the Synagogue* (London: Pitman & Sons, 1911), p. 451.
[9] Galatians 4:4.
[10] 2 Corinthians 5:21; 1 Peter 2:22.
[11] John 15:10.
[12] Talmud, *Seder Kodoshim, Mas. Menachoth* 39b.

[13] Alfred J. Kolatch. *The Jewish Book of Why* (Middle Village, N.Y.: Jonathan David Publishers, 1981), p. 100.

[14] Talmud. *Seder Nezakin, Mas. Baba Bathra* 98a.

[15] If a garment did not have four corners. it was exempted from the *mitzvah* to add *tzitzit.*

[16] Talmud, *Seder Nezakin, Mas. Baba Bathra* 57b.

[17] David Bivin. "The Hem of His Garment." *Jerusalem Perspective* (Issue 7, Apr., 1988), pp. 4-5.

[18] David Bivin. pp. 4-5.

[19] Rudolph Brasch. *The Judaic Heritage: Its Teachings, Philosophy, and Symbols* (New York: Van Rees Press, 1969). p. 236-238.

[20] Alan Unterman. *Jews: Their Religious Beliefs & Practices* (Boston: Routledge & Kegan Paul. Ltd., 1981), p. 140.

[21] *Zohar.* III:226.

[22] Rudolph Brasch, *The Judaic Heritage: Its Teachings, Philosophy, and Symbolism*, p. 239.

Chapter 3

A Mark of Remembrance

From the giving of the law at Sinai, the *tallit* had certain identifying characteristics that set the Jewish people apart as being chosen of God. What made it uniquely characteristic of the Jews was the fact that God required his chosen people to append one *tzitzit* (tassel) in each of the four corners of their outer garments. This is the commandment of the Torah: "Speak unto the children of Israel, and bid them that they make them fringes in the borders of their garments throughout their generations, and that they put upon the fringe of the borders [corners] a ribband of blue: and it shall be unto you for a fringe, that ye may look upon it, and remember all the commandments of the Lord, and do them; and that ye seek not after your own heart and your own eyes, after which ye use to go a whoring: that ye may remember, and do all my commandments, and be holy unto your God."[1]

This commandment is reiterated in the Fifth Book of Moses in a more concise form and without added explanation: "Make tassels on the four corners of the cloak you wear."[2] The implication of these statements is that when one looked upon the *tzitzit* he would remember God's commandments and seek after God's heart, not his own ways.

Most Christian theologians in history have faulted the Jewish people for their literalist interpretation of these and other passages, disparaging their faithfulness to do exactly what God had commanded them as "legalism" or an attempt to be justified before God "by works," rather than "by faith." All the while, the same theologians enjoin upon the church a literalist interpretation of Jesus' commandments, ". . .baptize them in the name of the Father, and of the Son, and of the Holy Spirit," or, "Take, eat; this is my body which is broken for you . . . take, drink; this is the blood of the new testament that is shed for the remission of sins," even teaching that salvation is gained or maintained through these sacramental institutions. The inconsistency is readily apparent: Jews are legalists because they attach *tzitziyot* to the corners of their garments, nail *mezuzot* to the door posts of their homes, or bind *tefillin* on their foreheads and arms; Christians freely exercise faith when they receive the sacraments of water of baptism or communion! Jews are legalists when they wear a *tallit*; Christian ministers manifest faith and devotion when they wear robes and stoles (which are descended directly from the *tallit*)!

The truth is that each of the practices that God enjoined upon the Jewish people was in perfect keeping with his continuing use of symbols and markings to single out and set apart times, places, and various material articles as semaphores directing his people's attention to his Word and commandments. God is a marking, identifying God. He establishes memorials to awaken in the hearts of his people memories of his great acts of deliverance and to generate faith for his continuing intervention in their behalf. Remembering God's mighty acts and his ongoing faithfulness to his covenants and his people is a manifestation of faith, not of legalism, of dependence upon God's loving-kindness (*chesed*), not upon human actions as means of acceptance before God. Remembrance and anamnesis (re-enactment) are central to worship both in Judaism and Christianity. Indeed, both faiths are centered in and function as calls to remembrance.

Due to the fact that men are finite and live within the constraints of time, they tend to forget things in the past. If markers are not placed to ensure remembrance, past events tend to be forgotten, particularly from generation to generation. Everyone laughs about tying a string around a finger so something will not be forgotten, but, in essence, God has done just that for his people at various times and in various places, creating markers in time, geography, and dress, both to single out his people as unique bearers of his name and to call to their remembrance his mighty acts on their behalf and his ongoing covenant with them.

More eloquent than words, a simple symbol speaks more powerfully than speech. This is why body language is more revealing than spoken words. As one walks through life, with all its pitfalls and diversions, symbols that demand his attention and restore the memory of his divine calling and its requirements are invaluable. Christianity is filled with these symbols: crosses, chalices, candles, paraments, banners, vestments, stained-glass windows, and the currently ubiquitous "WWJD" ("What Would Jesus Do?") emblems (which someone has called "Christian *tzitzit*"). For the Jew, the *tzitzit* of the *tallit* are silent, yet powerful symbols that point his heart to God.

Yitzhak Buxbaum described symbols this way: "If we deepen our devotion to God, and cultivate the habit,

many, many things will remind us of Him. For example, when you see an animal with horns, you will
be reminded of the *shofar* (the ram's horn) and of the
High Holidays and all they signify; or when you see a
body of water, you will be reminded of how God split
the Red Sea for our ancestors. This is a slight touch of
love-madness for God. As in the words of
[Maimonides], in our love for God we should be like
someone 'who is love-sick, and cannot take his mind
off the woman he loves.' "[3]

The concept of marking, singling out, or identifying is characteristic of God in another way. He places
marks on his people to signify their separation or sanc-
tification unto himself. His chosen people are not to be
like the other peoples of the earth. While they are not
to cloister themselves in a ghettoized existence isolated from the rest of the world, they are to be distinct
both in their conduct and in their appearance. This is
why God told Abraham, "Leave your country, your
people, and your father's household, and go to the
land I will show you."[4] This is the reason for his instruction to Moses: "You must not worship the Lord
your God in [the heathen's] way."[5] It was for this
reason that Jesus also implored the Father concerning
his disciples: "My prayer is not that you take them out
of the world but that you protect them from the evil
one."[6] This concept of being in the world but not of
the world has characterized God's Chosen People from
time immemorial. Often it has made them a
"gazingstock" for the secular and pagan societies in
which they have lived.

Because their unique lifestyle and appearance have
differed from societal norms, the Jewish people have
been targeted by those bureaucrats who have always

vented their frustration against anything that did not conform to societal norms with massive campaigns of persecution and violence. Persian Prime Minister Haman, the archetype for anti-Semitism, declared to his king: "There is a certain people . . . who keep themselves separate. Their customs are different from those of all other people . . . it is not in the king's best interests to tolerate them."[7]

God established parameters to limit his people's conduct and appearance both to keep them separate and to bear witness through the marks in their lifestyle and their persons to the fact that they were his chosen people, a testimony that he alone is God. The *tzitzit* tradition was one manifestation of God's spirit of marking that singled the Jewish people out as uniquely his and bore a public witness to the nations and peoples round about them that they were a God-dedicated people. The *tallit* was, in effect, a uniform that identified them as God's army, a force for peace and justice in the earth.

Through the ministry of Jesus, this uniform became the Holy Spirit himself, which clothed the believer "with power from on high," so that they could be witnesses to the living, incarnate Torah to "the ends of the earth."[8] The transition was from external material marking to internal spiritual marking, from an external uniform to a spiritual garment, the Holy Spirit. The effect, however, remained the same. God's people of all ages are to be singled out by markings that identify them in the world as his Chosen and serve as constant reminders that they are to fulfill his commandments and do his will. The *tallit* was such a mark of remembrance.

Following God's commandments and the leading

of his Spirit involves complete submission to the divine will, a total dependence upon God. The fringes that God required his people to attach to their garments reminded them not only of his commandments but also that they were not to live their lives after their own ways. Theirs were to be lives not only of obedience but also of trust, not only of submission but also of living faith.

In the wrappings, twistings, and knottings of the *tzitzit* is found the mystery of this principle. In Psalm 25:1-3, King David declared, "O my God, I trust in thee . . . let none that wait on thee be ashamed . . ." In Isaiah 40:31, the prophet declares that those who "wait upon the Lord shall renew their strength. . ." The word translated "wait" in these passages is קָוָה (*qavah*), which literally means "to twist, to bind as in a rope." It is also the normal verb "to hope," the root of which is seen in the Israeli National Anthem, *HaTikvah* (The Hope). Those who want to be successful in their relationship with God, mounting up with wings as eagles, will find themselves making a spiritual *tzitzit* daily by twisting, tying, and binding their lives together with the life of the Lord, thereby gaining the strength that is needed for victorious living. The Holy Spirit, indeed, is the *shamash*, the longest, helper strand of the *tzitzit* that binds the believers' lives together with the life of God. And, those who have wisdom will see that they are tightly wrapped in relationship with the God of the universe.[9]

The mantle (*tallit*) was not in itself unique to Israel. What was unique was the fact that it was to have "fringes" in its "borders." The Hebrew word for "fringe" is צִיצִת (*tzitzit*), which also means tassel or lock. The word for "border" is כָּנָף (*kanaph*), which primarily means wing, but also can be translated as corner or edge. This corresponds to the Greek description of Jesus' garment that is recorded in Mark 6:56: ". . . they . . . besought him that they might touch if it were but the border [κράσπεδον (*kraspedon*)] of his garment."

The *tzitzit* is also called גְדִיל (*gedil*), meaning intertwined threads or twisted work (cf. Greek: κράσπεδον, *kraspedon*, "twisted wool"). The *tzitzit* features a tassel of threads that are wrapped and knotted. Some have suggested that the knots were originally designed to indicate the binding of evil spirits as the *leitmotif* of tying and loosing knots was seen to parallel binding and loosing demons.[10] The written Torah, however, is not specific regarding the construction of *tzitzit*. Various traditions have specified different ways in which the threads are to be wrapped and knotted. The Karaites, who are not recognized as part of the Jewish community because of their fundamental biblicism and rejection of the "Oral Torah" tradition, knot the threads and literally make the *tzitzit* each

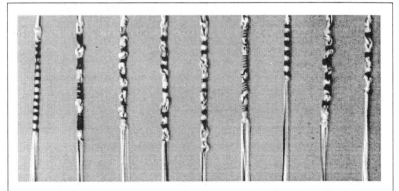

Some of the different traditions of tying *Tzitzit* *(P'Til Tekhelet Photo)*

time it is worn. When they are not wearing the *tzitzit*, it is hung in a prominent place in the home so that they may literally "look upon them" and be reminded of the *mitzvot*.

The Torah was very specific about the number and placement of the *tzitziyot* in the outer garment and about the purpose of their being so displayed. Deuteronomy 22:12 declares, "Make tassels on the four corners of the cloak you wear." There were to be four *tzitziyot*, with one set in each of the four corners of the cloak (כְּסוּת *kesuth*). The purpose for their placement was equally clear: ". . . that ye may look upon it, and remember all the commandments of the LORD, and do them."

Until this time, clothing for mankind had served only as a reminder of the sin of Adam and Eve when they rebelled against the one commandment which God had enjoined upon them. Indeed, the Hebrew word for garment (usually the outer garment or *tallit*) is בֶּגֶד (*beged*), which is derived from the verb root בָּגַד (*bagad*) meaning to rebel or to be faithless. Perhaps God had allowed the garment that he gave to cover man's nakedness to serve as a continuing reminder of his rebellion. Now, God took the symbol of sin and death and made it a reminder that he had set before Israel a choice between life and death, between blessing and cursing. The opportunity for life was found in faith toward God and obedience of his commandments that were vividly impressed upon their memories by the *tzitziyot* that were now to be appended to the four corners of their garments.

Metaphorically, the four corners of the *tallit* call to mind the four corners of the earth and the four directions, underscoring the fact that "the earth *is* the

Lord's, and the fulness thereof; the world, and they that dwell therein" and that "all the earth shall be filled with the glory of the Lord."[11] In whichever of the four directions the Jewish man turns, the *tzitzit* in that corner of his *tallit* makes him conscious of the omnipresent Creator and Lord of the universe.[12]

Rebbe Reb Zusya, of Hanipol, offered this suggestion for remembrance of the way of God: ". . .as soon as you wake up in the morning, take in your hand the holy *tzitzit* [many men wear their *tallit katan* while sleeping] and direct your mind and heart to meditate on the greatness and majesty of the Creator, blessed be He, and take on yourself the true fear of God–to have awe and fear because of His greatness. This should not be just a matter of rote and habit."[13]

There has never been a regulation in Judaism as to the size or length of the *tzitziyot*. Some five decades before Jesus' time, "The elders of the School of Shammai and the School of Hillel . . . reached the decision that there is no prescribed length for the tzitzit."[14] This, of course, led to some ostentatious displays by those whose devotion to God's Word knew no bounds and by those who wanted to appear more powerful and/or holy to the public than they actually were. One Jerusalem resident was remembered as being so devout that he was nicknamed, *"Ben Tsitsit HaKeset,"* because of his "long tassels that literally trailed behind him on the ground."[15] Though this man may well have been devout, there were others who merely made a hypocritical display that was condemned by Jesus in Matthew 23:5: "But all their works they do for to be seen of men: they make broad their phylacteries, and enlarge the borders [*tzitziyot*] of their garments." Though there were those who were thus deplored not only by Jesus but also by their fellow Pharisees, the vast majority of Jewish men in Jesus' day and in every generation before and after that time wore the *tallit* with *tzitziyot* with a pure heart, reminding them that they were to fulfill the commandments of the Eternal and not walk in their own ways.

Jewish men throughout history have been like the man described in the Talmud who did not yield to the temptation to commit an immoral act when he noticed the *tzitziyot* on his garment and was thus reminded that he would have to account to his Creator for the sin he contemplated.[16] The *tzitzit* has fulfilled God's design by summoning its wearer to recall the commandments of their God and to do them. For some, *tzitziyot* may have been a source of pride; however, for the vast majority of Jewish men in history they have been exactly what the Eternal designed them to be: constant visual reminders that their wearers were covenanted with God to remember all of his commandments and to observe them.

The Jewish people were to be a peculiar treasure unto God, a kingdom of priests who should love God with all their hearts, souls, and strength[17] and should manifest that love by fulfilling all of his commandments (*mitzvot*). Jesus was operating in complete accord with his own Jewish heritage when he made this same observation to his disciples: "If you love me, keep my commandments."[18]

A loving God designed a system of reminders to assist his chosen people in remembering his commandments and expressing their love to him: he provided visible markings in their clothing and elsewhere that constantly summoned them to obedience to his Word. This practice was no burden to the Jewish people but a privilege, a badge of honor through which one could visibly demonstrate his commitment to the Word of God.

[1] Numbers 15:38-40.
[2] Deuteronomy 22:12.
[3] Yitzhak Buxbaum, *Jewish Spiritual Practices* (Northvale, N.J.: Jason Aronson, Inc., 1990), p. 34.
[4] Genesis 12:1, NIV.
[5] Deuteronomy 12:4, NIV.
[6] John 17:15, NIV.
[7] Esther 3:8, NIV.
[8] Luke 24:49; Acts 1:8, NIV.
[9] This concept is amply illustrated in Karl D. Coke's audio teaching, "The Prayer Shawl," and in Doug Wheeler's "The Law of the Fringe," *Restore!* (Vol. 3, No. 2), pp. 28-32.
[10] W.O.E. Oesterly, p. 452.
[11] Psalm 24:1; Numbers 14:21.
[12] *Zohar*, III:175b.
[13] Rebbe Reb Zusya, quoted in Yitzhak Buxbaum, p. 84.
[14] *Sifre* Numbers 11:5, to 15:38, quoted in David Bivin, p. 5.
[15] David Bivin, p. 4. See Samuel Safrai, *The Jewish People in the First Century*, p. 798, note 3.
[16] Talmud, *Menachoth* 44a.
[17] Deuteronomy 6:5.
[18] John 14:15.

Chapter 4

A Ribband
of Blue

Literally and grammatically there was something more about the *tzitzit* that was to call Israel's attention to the commandments of God. In each *tzitzit* of each garment was to be a single ribband (thread) of blue. The Hebrew word for "ribband" is פְּתִיל (*petil*), meaning a cord or thread twisted into a fringe. It is perfectly described in the apostolic Greek κράσπεδον (*kraspedon*), "the appendage . . . made of twisted wool." Even more than the *tzitzit* itself, this single twisted blue thread was to be the reminder of God's *mitzvot*. Linguistically, the antecedent of the pronoun *it* (upon which Israelites were to look and remember) is "ribband" or the thread of blue. Since the word *tzitzit* is feminine and "it" ("You shall see *it*. . .") is masculine, the only antecedent possible is the thread of blue. The term for this "blue" in Hebrew is תְּכֵלֶת (*tekhelet*). Some sages have explained that the use of the masculine pronoun here may allude to an awareness of the Divine ("You shall see *him* [God] and remember").

The *tzitzit* was constructed of seven white strands of thread (a symbol for purity and pefection) entwined with the one blue thread, called the *shamash* or servant thread. The total of eight threads in the *tzitzit* manifests the number of new beginnings. The *tekhelet* thread, therefore, was the completion of the *tallit* and its *tzitziyot*. Its striking blue demanded the attention of its observer to the uniqueness of the fringe and its function.

In the ancient world, dyes that were both colorful and not subject to oxidation or fading were rare and costly. There was a particular fascination with colors in the spectrum ranging from crimson, through purple, to sky blue. These colors are frequently mentioned in the Bible as תְּכֵלֶת (*tekhelet*) "blue," אַרְגָּמָן (*'argaman*) "purple," and תּוֹלָע (*tola'*) "scarlet." The blue dye was derived from the hypobranchial gland of the *Murex trunculus* mollusk (sea snail), the purple from the hypobranchial gland of the *Thais haemastoma* sea mollusk, and the scarlet from the dried body of the female *coccus ilicis* worm or maggot. Each of these dyes was used to color fabrics that were essential parts of the tabernacle in the wilderness and in the temple.[1]

The dye for the color *tekhelet* was literally worth its weight in gold and more in the ancient world. As a matter of fact, wool dyed with *tekhelet* was worth up to twenty times its weight in gold.[2] One modern investigator demonstrated the high cost of *tekhelet* and purple dyes by finding it necessary to use over 8,500 such snails to obtain one gram of dye. Though a substitute dye, *kela ilan*, could be extracted from the Indian indigo plant, the best dye which did not fade or oxidize was taken from live mol-

Murex Trunculus sea mollusk, source of *tekhelet* (P'Til Tekhelet Photo)

lusks or sea snails.[3] It has been suggested that *tekhelet* dye from the *Murex trunculus* was one of the fastest dyes in the ancient world. (It binds very tightly to wool and will not fade over time.) It was probably for this reason that the Talmud specified that *tekhelet* for the *tzitzit* must come from a חִלָּזוֹן *(chilazon)*, which means any kind of land or sea snail in modern Hebrew[4] but probably referred to the *Murex trunculus* in ancient times. As the Talmud required, the *Murex trunculus* had a shell[5] and came from "between the ladders of Tyre and Haifa." The Talmud also specified that the dye be extracted from a live snail,[6] necessitating harvesting from the sea floor and immediately extracting the dye, as was the case with the *Murex trunculus*.

Because of their beauty, garments with these colors were in such demand that only the wealthy aristocracy and those of royalty could afford to wear them. Kings and emperors had their robes dyed in this "royal blue," or "royal purple." It was said that Cleopatra's sailing vessel had a sail of this blue. Due to the lucrative nature of purple and blue dyeing and the status conveyed by wearing such colors, there was much jockeying for control over the industry. The Romans brought the dyeing industry under imperial control, with Julius Caesar and Augustus Caesar restricting use of these dyes to the ruling classes.[7] Nero decreed that only the emperor had the right to wear blue or purple garments.[8] By the fourth century C.E., the Roman emperors decreed that these dyes be controlled wholly by the state.[9]

The most ancient of references to *tekhelet* is found in the Tell-el-Amarna Tablets (1500-1300 B.C.E.), where a "*sabâtu sâ takîltî*" (garment of *tekhelet*) was listed as one of the riches sent by the King of Mittani to the Egyptian prince as a dowry for his daughter.[10] Legend has it that the blue and purple dye was discovered when Hercules' dog bit into a *Murex* snail on the shores of Tyre, leaving his mouth stained purple. Tyrian coins from around 200 C.E. depict this legend, with the *Murex* clearly visible.[11]

Archaeological evidence suggests that the *tekhelet* dyeing process may have originated in Crete, where purple was being manufactured by Minoans as early as 1750 B.C.E.[12] Mounds of crushed *Murex trunculus* snails from around 1200 B.C.E. have been discovered at various sites between the promontory of Tyre in Lebanon and modern Haifa in Israel.[13] Historical references are made to this blue and purple dyeing process in the writings of Pliny the Elder[14] and Aristotle,[15] both of whom described the mollusks, where they could be located, and the procedure for dyeing with them.

From the archaeological and historical evidence there seems to be little doubt about the origin of the color *tekhelet*. Though some have suggested that it was extracted from the mollusks *Janthina pallida* and *Janthina bicolor*, most scholars agree that both *tekhelet* and *argaman* were extracted from *Murex* snails.[16]

Rediscovery of the dyeing process from the *Murex trunculus* snail has also helped clear the confusion between references to purple and blue in the ancient world. These terms were often used almost interchangeably so that "royal blue" was actually purple. Lydia, a merchant in "purple" was probably a seller of *tekhelet* (blue).[17]   When the secretion from the hypobranchial gland of the *Murex trunculus* mollusk is extracted, it is a clear, yellowish liquid, dibromoindigo, which is put into a reduced solution for vat dyeing wool. In the presence of sunlight, however, the ultraviolet spectrum causes the dibromoindigo to debrominate to indigo. The shade of the resultant color is dependent upon the degree of exposure to ultraviolet light; therefore, on a cloudy day or in controlled sunlight, the color is more violet or purple while on a cloudless day, the color is sky blue.

In Bible days, *tekhelet* was used in ancient Israel in garments for princes and nobles.[18] The High Priest's robe was entirely of *tekhelet*, and various fabrics used in the tabernacle and temple were of *tekhelet*. It was also used in fabrics for royal palaces.[19] The people of primitive Tyre were expert dyers with *tekhelet*,[20] and the tribe of Zebulun participated in this industry[21] as a part of its inheritance that included "the hidden treasures of the sands."[22] The Israelites under Deborah fought a war with the Canaanites that most likely involved this issue: ". . . to Sisera a prey of divers colours, a prey of divers colours of needlework, of divers colours of needlework on both sides, meet for the necks of them that take the spoil. . ."[23]

In the time of Jesus, the *tallit* with *tzitzit* with a thread of *tekhelet* was most certainly in use by Jewish men. It is likely that by that time an updated form of the ancient mantle was in popular use, perhaps even a precursor of the modern prayer shawl. At any rate, there can be no doubt but that the garment which Jesus wore as an integral part of his Torahcentric lifestyle was the *tallit* with *tzitzit* and *tekhelet*. His mantle was a rectangular woolen garment with a fringe appended and hanging down from each of its four corners, featuring a single strand of blue thread woven or twisted into each fringe. This was the "hem" of his garment which brought healing to "all who touched it."

Despite all the destruction of subsequent wars in

Israel and surrounding area, the *tekhelet* industry continued to produce the dye that was used to make the
distinctive marking in the outer garment of Jewish men
until at least 570 C.E., at the time of the redaction of
the Talmud. Rabbi Isaac Herzog suggests that the final
destruction of the Jewish *tekhelet* industry occurred
with the Arab conquest of Israel in 683 C.E.[24]

The secrets of *tekhelet* were then lost for perhaps
thirteen centuries, but they were rediscovered through
the dedication of enterprising rabbis, including Rav
Gershon Henokh Leiner of Radzyn, who thought that
it was derived from a squid's black secretion subjected
to heat and mixed with iron filings.[25] Rabbi Isaac
Herzog, first Chief Rabbi of the State of Israel, did
extensive research which disproved the Radzyn theory
and concluded that the *Murex* family was the likely
source of *tekhelet*. In 1985 Rabbi Eliahu Tavger of
Jerusalem began researching the ritual fringes and finally succeeded in exacting the process of dyeing with
tekhelet according to *halacha*. Today, after more than
1,300 years, *tzitzit* are again being made with a thread
dyed with *tekhelet* under the auspices of P'til Tekhelet,
a non-profit Israel-based organization that obtains
snails, extracts the dye, and dyes pure Merino wool.
These Israelis are among the many Jewish people in-
ternationally who have a passion for restoring ancient
materials and practices to Judaism, no doubt a part of
the spirit of restoration that is active in many faith
communities, both Jewish and Christian.

The majority of Jews today still use a prayer shawl
with plain white *tzitziyot*. Some prefer a blue stripe
across the *tallit* to recall the *tekhelet* thread while others employ a black stripe rather than the blue in remembrance of the destruction of the Temple. Increasing

numbers, however, are returning to the *tekhelet*-threaded *tzitzit*, the tradition of their ancient ancestors.

[1] Exodus 26:1, 31; 28:6.
[2] Baruch Sterman, *"Tekhelet"* (a paper posted on the Internet website of *P'til Tekhelet*, www.techeiles.org.il), p. 2.
[3] Talmud, *Seder Moed, Shabbat* 75a.
[4] *Shabbat* 26a; *Sifre* Deuteronomy 354.
[5] *Devarim Rabba* 67:ll; Talmud, *Seder Moed, Shabbat* 85a.
[6] Talmud, *Seder Moed, Shabbat* 85a
[7] Seutonius, *Vita Caes*, p. 43.
[8] *Vita Neronis*, p. 32.
[9] J. T. Baker, "Tyrian Purple: an Ancient Dye, a Modern Problem," (*Endeavor*, 33, 1974), pp. 11-17.
[10] Samuel Mercer, *The Tell El-Amarna Tablets* (Macmillan, 1939), p. 85.
[11] Baruch Sterman, p. 2.
[12] Robert Stieglitz, "The Minoan Origin of Tyrian Purple," (*Biblical Archaeologist*, 57:1, 1994), pp. 46-54.
[13] J. B. Pritchard. *Recovering Sarepta, A Phoenician City* (Princeton: Princeton University Press, 1978), p. 38.
[14] Pliny the Elder, *Natural History*, Book IX, LX-LXV.
[15] Aristotle, *De Animalibus Historia*, p. 175.
[16] Encyclopaedia Judaica: *"Tekhelet."*
[17] Acts 16:14.
[18] Ezekiel 23:6.
[19] Esther 1:6.
[20] 2 Chronicles 2:7; Ezekiel 27:7.
[21] According to the *midrash* of Talmud, *Seder Moed, Mas. Megiluh.* 6a.
[22] Deuteronomy 33:19.
[23] Judges 5:30.
[24] Isaac Herzog. *The Royal Purple*, p. 114. Quoted in Baruch Sterman, p. 5.
[25] See Baruch Sterman, p. 6.

Chapter 5

Tzitzit and Tekhelet

Considering the exorbitant cost of *tekhelet* dye, why would God require every Israeli male to display a thread of this blue in each corner of his mantle (*tallit*)? And, considering the difficulty and cost of constructing fringes and attaching them to the outer garment, why would God consider it important for his people to make such a display? The *tzitziyot* are certainly not essential to the structural integrity of the garment and are of no material benefit.

For the Jewish man, the blue thread in the *tzitzit* was a reminder of God himself. Rabbi Meir spoke thus about the *tekhelet* thread in the *tzitzit* of the *tallit*: "Why was the color blue chosen from all the other colors? Because the blue resembles the sea, the sea resembles the sky, and the sky resembles the Throne of Glory."[1] God's throne is described biblically as "like sapphire stone, and as the sky itself for clearness."[2] Very often in Jewish history and practice, God himself is referred to by the euphemism *heaven*, so as not to say "God" in any way that might show disrespect for his holiness. This was the case in the ministry of Jesus as reported in the Gospel of Matthew where the term *kingdom of heaven* is used instead of *kingdom of God* as in the other gospels. When a Jewish man in biblical times looked at the *tzitzit* in the corners of his mantle, he saw a blue thread that reminded him of heaven and the sapphire throne of God.

The thread of *tekhelet* (blue) was to be exactly the same color of the high priest's robe, which was "all of blue."[3] The other elements of the high priest's garments were decorated with *tekhelet* as well as with gold, purple, and scarlet (crimson). The official uniform, then, in which the high priest approached the service of the Tabernacle was "all of *tekhelet*" with various other accents. This fact is very important when one considers its implications when applied to each Jewish man's *tallit*.

Jacob Milgrom has succinctly stated what has long been believed among the Jews as God's reason for requiring a blue thread in each man's *tzitzit*. He noted that "the democratic thrust within Judaism which equalizes not by leveling but by elevating" is manifest in the *tekhelet* of the *tzitzit*. "All of Israel is enjoined to become a nation of priests," he wrote. Since in ancient times *tekhelet* was the outward sign of nobility and of priesthood, God required the Jews to wear this blue woolen cord as a sign that in Israel he had "combined nobility with priesthood" so that Israel was "not to rule man but to serve God." *Tekhelet* in the *tzitzit* was not restricted to kings, priests, sages, or rabbis. "It is the uniform of all Israel," Milgrom noted.[4]

Rudolph Brasch has made this observation regarding the *tallit* as Israel's uniform: "The Jew's battle is not that of bloodshed. He serves the King of Kings. His fight is more difficult since he strives not for tangible conquests, but for the values of the spirit. To identify himself as God's soldier and to make himself recognizable as such to the world, he dons his uniform, the *tallit*. Its whiteness symbolizes the purity of his mission."[5]

Perhaps another reason that God made this requirement was to emphasize the fact that every man in Israel as the head of a family had the responsibility of being both king and priest in his home. He was to lead his family in worship of God and in the priestly act of extending God's providential blessings upon both his wife and children, the same blessings that God instructed Aaron to place upon all the children of Israel.[6] When any Jew saw the blue thread in his *tzitzit*, he was immediately reminded that he was a part of that "kingdom of priests" that God had uniquely called unto himself.[7] The Israelites were commanded to place a thread of blue in the *tzitzit* of their *tallit* because they understood themselves to be "*banim la-Makom*, noble sons of the King of the Universe, always pursuing His *mitzvot*,"[8] an understanding that remains to this day.

The second reason for the *tekhelet* in the *tzitzit* was so that "ye may look upon it, and remember all the commandments of the Lord, and do them." Both the *tzitzit* and the *tekhelet* are physical reminders of all the commandments of God, encouraging Jews to "do them." This passage that requires the placement of *tzitzit* and *tekhelet* in the garments of Jews is a part of the *kri'at ha-Shema* prayer complex that is recited twice daily by observant Jews; therefore, it is a constant reminder of the commandments. This call to remembrance and observance of the commandments is manifest in the *tzitzit* of the *tallit* on three different levels, first with the *Shema* (the greatest commandment), then with the Decalogue (Ten Commandments), and finally with the sum total of all the commandments (*mitzvot*).

The most important commandment in the entire Word of God is the *Shema*: "Hear, O Israel, the Lord our God, the Lord is One: and thou shalt love the Lord thy God with all thy heart, and with all thy soul, and with all thy mind, and with all thy strength." Jesus, himself, confirmed the fact that this was the first and greatest commandment.[9] Allusions to each of the Ten Commandments can also be found in the *Shema*; however, the most important declaration in the *Shema* is this: "The Lord is One."In Hebrew, this phrase is יהוה אֶחָד (*Y-H-W-H Echad*). The Hebrew for "The Lord" (יהוה) is commonly written by Jews as 'ה or " in order not to desecrate the Holy Name.[10]

Each letter in the Hebrew alphabet has a numerical equivalent, so that א (*aleph* [a]) is 1, ב (*beth* [b]) is 2, ג (*gimel* [g]) is 3, and so forth. When the corresponding numbers for the Hebrew letters in *Y-H-W-H* (י+ה+ו+ה) are added, the sum is 26; therefore, the

THE LORD IS ONE

י	=	10	=	Y
ה	=	5	=	H
ו	=	6	=	W
ה	=	5	=	H

Y-H-W-H (The Lord)
=
26

א	=	1	=	E
ח	=	8	=	CH
ד	=	4	=	D

ECHAD (One)
=
13

–Table design by Karl D. Coke

word *Y-H-W-H* numerically equals 26 (see chart). When the corresponding numbers for אֶחָד are added, the sum is 13 (see chart).

These numbers (and their corresponding Hebrew words) are seen in the *tzitzit* in the following manner: The *tzitzit* (tassel) has five double knots (corresponding to the Pentateuch, the five books of Moses) with four sets of wrappings between them. The first three sets of wrappings total 26 (set one: 7 wrappings; set two: 8 wrappings; set three: 11 wrappings). 26 is the numerical equivalent of God's own personal name (*Y-H-W-H*). Even more specifically, 7 + 8 = 15, the equivalent of ה+י (Y+H), and 11 is the equivalent of ה+ו (W+H). Then, the fourth set of wrappings totals 13, the numerical equivalent of אֶחָד (*echad*), "one" (see chart). When an observant Jew, then, looks

The Tzitzit

——— Knot #1

——— 7 Wrappings

——— Knot # 2

——— 8 Wrappings

——— Knot #3

——— 11 Wrappings

——— Knot #4

——— 13 Wrappings

——— Knot # 5

——— 8 Threads

–Table design by Karl D. Coke

upon the *tzitzit* of his prayer shawl, he first sees the numbers 26 and 13, which correspond precisely to אֶחָד 'ה (*Y-H-W-H Echad*, "the Lord is one"), the essential

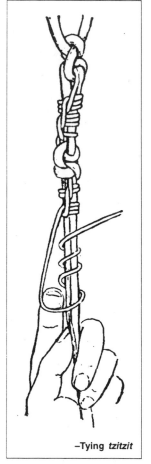

words of the greatest of all commandments, the *Shema*.

When he looks upon the *tzitzit* with *tekhelet*, the praying man also sees the Decalogue, the two tablets containing the Ten Commandments. *Mishnat Rabbi Eliezer*, chapter 14 says, "And the Rabbis said: Why does the Torah enjoin us regarding *tekhelet*? Because *tekhelet* resembles sapphire, and the Tablets were of sapphire, to tell you that so long as the people of Yisrael gaze upon this *tekhelet* they are reminded of that which is inscribed on the Tablets and they fulfill it, and so it is written, 'And you shall see it and remember.' "[11] By seeing the blue in the *tzitzit*, the Jewish man remembers the two tablets upon which the fiery finger of God himself wrote the Decalogue, the ten commandments that are the categories under which all other commandments are delineated.

–Tying *tzitzit*

The *Zohar* also notes that the word *tekhelet* means "*takhlit*," the "absolute and ultimate end and object of everything (viz. the *Shekhinah*)".[12]

As a Jewish man looks upon the *tzitzit* of his *tal-*

lit, he also sees the sum total of the *mitzvot*. Rashi, the great eleventh century Jewish commentator, explained how looking at the fringes reminds the Jewish man of all God's commandments, not just the Decalogue (as noted above). Again, using the fact that the letters of the Hebrew alphabet have numerical equivalents, Rashi explained that the Hebrew word צִיצִית[13] (*tzitzit*) is numerically equivalent to 600 (צ [90] + י [10] + צ [90] + י [10] + ת [400] = 600) and that the *tzitzit* are comprised of a total of 8 strings, tied with 5 knots, making a total of 13. When these numbers are added together, the sum is 613, the exact number of commandments (*mitzvot*) in the Torah.[14]

It should also be noted that there are 365 negative commandments (the "thou shalt not's"), corresponding to the number of days in a year, and 248 positive commandments (the "thou shalt's"), corresponding to the number of days remaining in a year after all sabbaths and holy days have been subtracted. The Jewish people also traditionally count 248 bones in the human body, held together by 365 ligaments.

The 613 *mitzvot* are also manifest in the blue thread of the *tzitzit*, in the very color *tekhelet* itself. As two Belgian scientists recently studied characteristics of dye molecules obtained from the *Murex trunculus* sea mollusk, they made a startling discovery. One of the measurements was the absorption spectrum of the molecule. Light is made up of many colors (the spectrum) measured in units of nanometers. The human eye perceives color in a complex way, based on the various combinations of colors of light that strike it. The *tekhelet* molecule (indigotin) gets its color from a strong absorption peak centered at exactly 613 nanometers![15]

When an observant Jewish man looks upon and touches to his eyes the *tzitzit* of his *tallit* (prayer shawl), he recognizes the *Shema* (the first and greatest commandment), the Ten Commandments, and the 613 *mitzvot*. Furthermore, he is constantly reminded to do them, thereby submitting himself to the Word and will of God.

Since a blue thread stands for the Torah or the Word of God, is it perhaps more than mere coincidence that the color *blue* has long been associated with truth. Who does not recognize the phrase *true blue* as a statement that something or someone is profoundly correct or faithful? Is it coincidence that the most outstanding example in any contest receives the "blue ribbon" award?

The *tallit* with its *tzitziot* and *tekhelet* is a curious, unique tradition, part of God's grand design of mnemonic devices to call his people to the remembrance of his mighty acts on their behalf and to the expression of their devotion to him; however, it has fulfilled its function for over 3,500 years and to this day still calls observant Jews back to Sinai and the presence of God's Torah.

---

[1] Talmud. *Seder Nashim, Mas. Sotah* 17a.
[2] Exodus 24:10.
[3] Exodus 28:31.
[4] Jacob Milgrom. "The Tassel and the Tallit" (Fourth Annual Rabbi Louis Fineberg Memorial Lecture, University of Cincinnati, 1981).
[5] Rudolph Brasch, *The Judaic Heritage: Its Teachings, Philosophy, and Symbolism*, p. 239.
[6] Numbers 6:24, 25.
[7] Exodus 19:16.
[8] See *P'til Tekhelet* (Internet website: www.techeiles.org.il), p. 2.
[9] Mark 12:29, 30.
[10] 'ה is commonly used among the Jewish people to indicate the Tetragrammaton (four-letter name of God) that appears throughout the Hebrew Scriptures. The

name is spelled in Hebrew *yôdh, heh, waw, heh.* Where the Tetragrammaton is used in the Hebrew text of Scripture, it is vowel-pointed thus ה/ְ/ה/ֲ, using the vowels of the word *Adonai* (Lord), so that it may be pronounced, "*Adonai*." This time-honored tradition that predates the days of Jesus shows ultimate respect for the personal name of God by not permitting its use. It also reflects the Jewish people's attempt to avoid violation of the third commandment of the Decalogue: "Thou shalt not take the name of the Lord thy God in vain." Jesus himself respected this tradition by using "kingdom of heaven" instead of "kingdom of God," substituting "heaven" as a euphemism for "God," just as all Jews do, using "*Adonai*" for the Tetragrammaton, and as many do, using "*HaShem*" (The Name) instead of "God." It is important that Christians understand the fact that God does have a personal name. That name is Y/H/W/H. A close, yet inaccurate translation/transliteration of this personal name has appeared as *Jehovah*. This rendering repeats the mistake made by the late Renaissance Christian Hebraists when they saw *yôdh, heh, waw, heh* in the Masoretic Hebrew text with the *nekudot* (vowel pointing) of the Hebrew word *Ad̲o̲na̲i̲* (Lord) supplied (vowels emphasized). Since in German the letter "y" corresponds to "j" and "w" corresponds to "v," the transliteration became *Yehowah* or *Yehovah*, which came into English as *Jehovah*. Though Jehovah is etymologically incorrect, it is a cultural English (or other language) equivalent of *HaShem* that can (some would argue, should) be used by Christians to avoid pronunciation of the Tetragrammaton. In respect to our Jewish friends, we have noted the Tetragrammaton as here 'ה.

[11] See *P'til Tekhelet* (Internet website: www.techeiles.org.il), p. 1.

[12] *Zohar*, III:175b, 226b.

[13] In the third paragraph of the *Shema* (Numbers 15:38-39), *tzitzit* is צצת, which is "defective," without the final *yôdh*. Elsewhere it is written "*plene*" with the final *yôdh*.

[14] For a detailed discussion of this concept, cf. Karl D. Coke. "Prayer Lessons from Jewish Culture," *Restore!*, Vol. 4, No. 3.

[15] James Kern, "Tsitsit and Tekhelet" (an unpublished paper).

Chapter 6

Under
His Wings

Some Jewish *Siddurim* (prayer books) have a meditation to be said after a Jewish man puts on the *tallit*, while it fully covers the head and eyes. Quoting from Psalm 36:7 this prayer suggests the full significance of the *tallit*: "How precious is thy loving-kindness, O God! And under the shadow of thy wings do the children of men take shelter. . ." As an observant Jewish man covers himself with his *tallit*, he has a physical symbolic awareness of the fact that he is secure in the shadow of God's presence. He is "under the wings" of the Almighty. "When you put on a *tallit* you should think that the Light of the Infinite One is hidden within this *tallit* that you wrap yourself in . . . and that when the wings of the *tallit* cover you, you are covered in the wings of the Light of the Infinite One."[1]

The reason for this belief is that the Hebrew word for the corner of the *tallit*, כָּנָף (*kanaph*), also means "wing." As a practical demonstration, when a Jewish man dons his *tallit*, holding the *tzitzit* in the corners of the *tallit*, he can take on the appearance of being winged by merely raising his arms. The corners extended upward and outward demonstrate wings. Of course, God, himself, certainly cannot be anthropo-

morphized and does not literally have the physical features of any of his creation; however, in order for human beings to understand his nature more clearly, he
permits man to think of him in anthropomorphic terms.
Paul elucidates this truth in Romans 1:20: "For the
invisible things of [God] from the creation of the world
are clearly seen, being understood by the things that
are made, even his eternal power and Godhead; so
that [men] are without excuse. . ." What God has created and what man has made through God's inspiration may be used to help us understand the nature and
attributes of God.

So it is with the *tallit* for every Jewish man in
history who has used it in prayer. For the ancient agrarian
people, all of the powerful imagery of a mother hen's
taking her chicks under her wings when danger is
present came vividly to mind when they wrapped themselves in their mantles with *tzitziot* in the corners. They
knew that God's Torah, symbolized by the *tzitzit*, was
their guardian, his divine provision for their protection. They knew that they were God's children and
that like the chicks of a mother hen, they were shel-
tered under the protecting wings of the Almighty: "He
that dwelleth in the secret place of the most High shall
abide under the shadow of the Almighty . . . He shall
cover thee with his feathers, and under his wings shalt
thou trust. . ."[2] Again, the word for "wings" in this
powerful passage is כָּנָף (*kanaph*), the corners of the
tallit. It is, therefore, easy to visualize God's protec-
tive power enshrouding one when he is covered with
the four corners of the *tallit*.

For Jews of every age, there has been a distinct
understanding that God overshadowed them with his
presence and that his Torah was a guardian for them.

Paul, the Pharisee and apostle of Jesus Christ, made such a distinct comparison in Galatians 3:24: "Wherefore the Torah was our guardian to bring us unto Messiah, that we might be justified by faith" (literal translation). Paul's observation has profound implications: the law of God (Torah) is a παιδαγωγός (*paidagogos*) to bring "us" (both Jews and Gentiles) to Messiah. A *paidagogos* in Greek culture was a servant entrusted as a guardian of a wealthy family's children. It was the duty of this slave to teach proper etiquette and social skills to the children and to see that they were escorted to their teacher.

The parallel between the work of Torah and the Greek *paidagogos* is underscored when we consider that the Greek word νόμος (*nomos*) that translates the word *Torah* in the Septuagint version of the Hebrew Scriptures (and in the Apostolic Writings) is likely an adaptation of the Aramaic word *namosa* or the Semitic root *nemus* both of which mean "to civilize." (In modern Hebrew, נמוס (*nimmus*) means "polite or well-mannered behavior.") The word *nomos* principally means "teaching or instruction, and only secondarily law." It can be seen in English words like astronomy (instruction about the stars) and agronomy (instruction about fields).

When *nomos* was translated into Latin, the word *lex* (genitive: *legis*, from which we get the English word *legislation*) was used both in the *Vetus Latina* and Jerome's Vulgate, and a decided shift in semantics began to disparage God's divine instruction (*Torah*). It became "the law" in a juridical construct rather than "instruction" in a pedagogical construct.

In Paul's view, then, the Torah was and remains a guardian to teach all men how to conduct themselves in a civilized, polite, and well-mannered way in the presence of God and of man and to escort them to faith in the Messiah, the Teacher of teachers.

Jews have recognized the fact that God's law, symbolized in the *tzitzit* of their prayer shawls, is their guardian. Just as the *tallit* surrounds the praying Jew, so God surrounds his people. "We can intend when putting on the *tallit* that it separate us and shield us from outside distractions and from foreign thoughts. The large prayer *tallit* surrounds one and this symbolizes protection."[3] When a Jewish man wraps himself in his *tallit*, he symbolically places himself under God's sheltering love. Indeed, when he dons the *tallit*, he recites Psalm 36:7, 9: "How excellent *is* thy lovingkindness, O God! therefore the children of men put their trust under the shadow of thy wings. . . . For with thee *is* the fountain of life: in thy light shall we see light." This material action gives new and more intimate meaning to Psalm 57:1's declaration: "In the shadow of thy wings will I make my refuge."

In the centerpiece of material manifestation of God's religion for his chosen people is a demonstration of God's provision for, and protection of, his people. The ark of the covenant that was the focal point of the "Most Holy Place" in both the tabernacle in the wilderness and the temple in Jerusalem demonstrates the fact that even God's throne itself is overshadowed by the wings of divine protection (in this case, a shielding from view of the awesome presence of the Almighty). The mercy seat on the top of the ark of the covenant was the site of the localized material manifestation of the Spirit of God, the *Shekhinah*. Covering the four corners of the mercy seat were the wings of two cherubim. What powerful imagery: God's provision of mercy and loving kindness for his people is always overshadowed and protected by the wings of the "living creatures" that both guard his throne and extend perpetual, unceasing worship that extols his holiness: "*Kadosh, kadosh, kadosh*" ("Holy, holy, holy").[4] The testimony to God's ancient people (and to his people of all ages) is that his mercies are unending, extending to the age of the ages.[5] Those in the Messiah, the *soma tou Christou* (the body of the Christ) are "seated with Christ in heavenly places"[6] enfolded in the wings of his everlasting mercies.

The very basis of this redeemed status, this quality of being chosen of God to be in covenant with him, is established on God's overshadowing presence that makes atonement, pardons sin, and imparts the divine presence in an intimacy that can only be compared with marriage. Israel was espoused in marriage to God himself at Sinai when the people agreed to accept the commandments of the Torah and to obey God's Word. The church is espoused as the bride of Christ in that divine act of grace when sins are forgiven, righteousness is imputed for faith, and the New Covenant joins the believer in intimacy with the living Lord.[7] The salvation from the Jews[8] that has come to the nations through the person and work of Jesus Christ is based in God's providing a covering for the sins of mankind.

From the very beginning, when Adam and Eve first sinned and brought judgment upon the entire human race, God provided skins as a covering for their nakedness by sacrificing an animal. Later, at the time of delivering Israel from Egyptian slavery, God directed Moses to require the sacrifice of a lamb from each household, with the blood of the lamb applied to the door posts and lintels of their houses. This was to be the Passover (*Pesach*), meaning "to jump over." Later the mercy seat כַּפֹּרֶת (*kaporet*) of the ark of the covenant was literally the "place of covering." The annual Day of Atonement when the high priest made sacrifice for his own sins and for the sins of all Israel was כִּפּוּר יוֹם (*Yom Kippur*), the "day of covering." Both *kaporet* and *kippur* come from the root which means "to cover."

In atonement, God literally covers the sin of man with the blood of the Lamb so that those sins may be blotted out and man may be brought to a state of righteousness with which the holiness of God may have communion. For Israel, it began with covering their households with the sacrifice that permitted the angel of death to pass over their houses and spare their first-born, and it has been renewed each year on the "day of covering," the Day of Atonement. For Christians, it was initiated in the sacrifice of Jesus as the Paschal Lamb of God, a once-and-for-all atonement that is applied to each believing heart upon the confession of faith in God's provision through Christ. It is renewed continually as the believer confesses his sins, appeals to the Advocate with the Father, and receives the impartation of grace.[9] In every respect, each believer, whether Jew or Gentile, is under the shadow of the Almighty's wings, wholly dependent upon God's grace and mercy for the forgiveness of his sins, the imputation of righteousness, the impartation of life, and the continuation of divine protection. They are under his wings!

It is very likely that Jesus appealed to this powerful imagery of the overshadowing wings of divine protection when he lamented concerning his extended Jewish family: "O Jerusalem, Jerusalem . . . how often would I have gathered thy children together, even as a

hen gathereth her chickens under her wings . . ."[10]
Those Israelites who heard these words would have
immediately recognized the imagery, whether or not
Jesus made an actual demonstration with outstretched
arms. As the Messiah, it was his will even then to
extend the provision and protection of the Eternal to
all of his brethren according to the flesh. He would at
that time have fulfilled the Messianic promise to all of
Israel as the "Sun of righteousness" rising with "healing in his wings."[11] Just as he had extended healing to
the woman and the people of Gennesaret, he would
have extended peace and protection to all of Israel.
And, indeed, in his own time he will come out of Zion
to turn away ungodliness from Jacob,[12] and he will
fully enfold his own kinsmen in the shadow of his
tallit.

[1] *Or ha-Ganuz l.Tzaddikim,* p. 36, quoted in Yitzhak Buxbaum, p. 106.
[2] Psalm 91:1, 4.
[3] Yitzhak Buxbaum, p. 106.
[4] Isaiah 6:3.
[5] Psalm 107:1.
[6] Ephesians 2:6.
[7] Romans 5:1, 2; 7:4; 8:1-17.

Chapter 7

A Symbol
of Authority

Because the *tzitzit* was designed by God to call every Jewish man to remembrance of all the commandments of the Torah, the very Word of God, it came to symbolize authority. The degree of one's recognized authority in the community could often be gauged by observing the size of the *tzitzit* on his mantle. It was against such ostentatious displays of the wealthy aristocracy of Jewish society that Jesus directed his deprecation: "Everything they do is done for men to see: they make their phylacteries [*tefillin*] wide and the tassels on their garments long . . ."[1] Regardless of how men of pride may have abused this practice, it still remains that the *tzitzit* was recognized as a symbol of the authority of God and of its wearer.

One prime example of this can be seen in an event that occurred in the life of Samuel, the prophet whom God used first to anoint and then to judge Israel's first king, Saul. The king had disobeyed God's specific commandment and then had sought to make a sacrifice as a means of covering up for his sin of disobedience, prompting Samuel's famous pronouncement: ". . .to obey is better than sacrifice, and to hearken than the fat of rams."[2] As Samuel turned from pronouncing God's judgment upon Saul, the king grasped at the "skirt of [Samuel's] mantle, and it rent." A more accurate translation of this statement would aid in its interpretation: ". . . he caught the corner of [Samuel's] mantle, and it tore." The word *skirt* is actually כָּנָף (*kanaph*), which means "wing" or "corner." In the corner of each mantle was a *tzitzit*. It was the *tzitzit* which Saul grasped, and in his desperation ripped, from the corner of Samuel's *tallit*, or mantle. In this case, the word for mantle is מְעִיל (*me'il*), which meant a robe, a garment worn over a tunic by men of rank.

Samuel made this prediction on the basis of Saul's act of ripping the *tzitzit* from the corner of his mantle: "The Lord hath rent the kingdom of Israel from thee this day, and hath given it to a neighbour of thine, that is better than thou." Just as Saul had grasped and torn the outward symbol of Samuel's authority with God, so God would remove the monarchial dynasty from the house of Saul and give it to another. Just as the very act of ripping the *tzitzit* from the *tallit* rendered it ceremonially invalid (*pasul*), so Saul's leadership of Israel would be invalid.

Another example that illustrates this same principle also occurred in the life of Saul. Following Saul's rejection by God, he became virtually insane trying to protect that which God had already taken from him, his authority. In his jealous anger, he sought to kill David, the man whom God had anointed as his successor. One day Saul entered a cave in the wilderness of En Gedi where David and his men were hiding. In an impetuous act of bravado, David "cut off the skirt of Saul's robe."[3] This passage should be translated, "David . . . cut off the corner of Saul's robe." Again, the word for corner is כָּנָף (*kanaph*), which places the emphasis on the *tzitzit* that were always in the corners of Israelite garments. David had cut one of the *tzitziot* from Saul's robe.

No sooner had David completed this act than his conscience smote him, prompting him to repent for having done such a brazen thing. Symbolically, he had removed the sign of Saul's authority, seizing what had not yet fully become his own. He lamented: "The Lord forbid that I should do this thing unto my master, the Lord's anointed, to stretch forth mine hand against him, seeing he is the anointed of the Lord." Subsequently he called the action to Saul's attention, underscoring the fact that even when he had opportunity he would not take by force of violence what in due time God himself would deliver into his hands.

The recognition of authority manifest in the *tzitzit* in both of these events was not because the *tzitzit* possessed any magical powers but because of what it symbolized: "When you look upon it, remember my Torah," God had said. The *tzitzit* was a visible symbol that called to mind the Word of God, the ultimate source of all authority in the universe. The Word of God embodied in the Torah is "alive and powerful."[4]

Is it any wonder, then, that the woman and the multitudes of Gennesaret were healed when they reached out to touch the *tzitzit* on Jesus' *tallit*? There, they saw the visible symbol of the Word of God, the undergirding of all authority. This action may seem to have been superstitious to an uninformed observer; however, in the rich tradition of the Jewish people, it was a natural thing to do: touch the one part of the Rabbi's clothing that symbolized the Word of God (Torah) and the authority that God had given to him as the Son of Man. And the results were both astounding and expected. God delivered those who believed, not in some magic in the *tzitzit*, but in the power of the Word of God that created and sustains all things. The miracles involved the release of a minuscule portion of the "all power" (ἐξουσὶα, *exousia*), the authority given to Jesus in heaven and in earth.[5] The people's faith was in the one God who is יִרְאֶה 'ה[6] (*Y-H-W-H yir'eh*), the God who sees and provides.[7] When they touched the Rabbi's *tzitzit*, they grasped the totality of God's commandments and, in effect, the very essence of all that God, himself, is.

[1] Matthew 23:5, NIV.
[2] 1 Samuel 15:22.
[3] 1 Samuel 24:4.
[4] Hebrews 4:12.
[5] Matthew 28:18.
[6] See note 10, p. 60.
[7] Genesis 22:14.

Chapter 8

The Mantle Passes

A most unique story that demonstrates the authority that is manifest in the *tallit* and particularly in the *tzitzit* is found in the prophet Elijah's appointment of Elisha to be his successor. As he neared the end of his illustrious career as a champion of monotheistic faith, Elijah had fled from the face of Jezebel unto Mount Sinai, where he had hidden himself in a cave. Upon hearing the voice of God inquiring, "What are you doing here?", Elijah went to the entrance of the cave and "wrapped his face in his mantle."[1]

The mantle that Elijah wore was an אַדֶּרֶת (*'adderet*), a cloak (made of fur or fine material) or a prophet's garment. Since Elijah was a Torah-observant Jew, it is clear that the mantle that he wore was the ancient *tallit*, with the *tzitziot* in the four corners. In his subsequent conversation with the Lord, Elijah remained in this condition, with his face covered with his "mantle." Elijah wrapped himself in his *tallit* as he conversed with God. It was not unusual then or now for a Jewish man to cover his face when he communed with God. Then, as now, the enshrouded worshipper was alone with God, focused entirely on his divine purposes.

As Elijah stood in the entrance of the cave with

his head covered by his *tallit*, he heard the voice of God specifically instructing him to ". . . anoint Elisha . . . to succeed you as prophet." Then Elijah was told that even though he was alone in the cave of Sinai, God had "seven thousand in Israel–all whose knees have not bowed down to Baal."[2]

Another significant event involving Elijah's *tallit* occurred in the subsequent calling, anointing, and commissioning of Elisha. When Elijah found Elisha plowing with twelve yoke of oxen, he passed by him and threw his *tallit* (mantle, cloak) upon him. The impact of this act was immediate and profound. The young man left his oxen, kissed his mother and father goodbye, returned to slaughter his oxen and burn his plowing equipment, gave the meat to the people, and followed Elijah as his attendant.

There was something more than mere symbolism in Elijah's act of passing his mantle to Elisha. When the young plowboy was enveloped in Elijah's *tallit*, an immediate and lasting change occurred in his life. Perhaps the symbol of authority manifest in the *tzitziot* in the four corners of the prophet's mantle brought to the young man's mind the commandments of God and their power and impact upon all of Israel. Perhaps he remembered how Elijah had championed monotheism and the worship of God in Israel.

At any rate, Elisha's mind was riveted upon the obvious call that God had placed upon his life, and his eyes were fastened upon the grizzled old prophet who for so long had maintained such a profound reputation for his devotion to the one true God in the face of an idolatrous political system and a generally wayward populace. The *tzitziyot* on the prophet's *tallit* were an obvious physical manifestation of the amazing power resident in the prophet by the Holy Spirit. As that authority enshrouded Elisha, he knew that he would never be the same, and he made provisions to fulfill God's call upon his life.

Apparently, great significance was attached to Elijah's *tallit*, for in a subsequent event it was used as an instrument in an extraordinary miracle. "And Elijah took his mantle, and wrapped *it* together, and smote the waters, and they were divided hither and thither, so that they two went over on dry ground."[3] The prophet's *tallit* was used as a means of demonstrating God's power. There was no small amount of significance attached to the fact that in the corners of the garment were *tzitziyot* which said to the prophet who used it and to all the Israelis who saw it: "Remember all the commandments of the Lord, and do them; and that ye seek not after your own heart and your own eyes."

The parting of the Jordan was another in a series of events that tested Elisha's determination to receive a "double portion" of Elijah's spirit. Though many profound miracles had been performed in the course of Elijah's prophetic ministry, perhaps his most important years came in the twilight of his career when he became Elisha's mentor. The young student (*talmid*) was literally covered with the dust of his teacher as he followed him with all diligence. Though Elijah repeatedly discouraged Elisha from following him, the student prophet vowed, "As the Lord liveth, and as thy soul liveth, I will not leave thee."[4]

When Elijah was subsequently taken up into heaven by the whirlwind of a chariot and horses of fire, his *tallit* fell from him. Elisha took up that symbol of prophetic authority and returned to the Jordan

River where he smote the waters just as Elijah had done. The moment the *tzitziyot* touched the surface of the Jordan, the waters parted, and Elisha passed over on dry ground. The astounded sons of the prophets then observed: "The spirit of Elijah doth rest on Elisha."[5] They could clearly see that the mantle had passed and that the authority that had covered Elijah now rested upon Elisha. There was no magic in the mantle; however, it was a material channel for demonstrating the power of God's Word that he had breathed into the prophet's life. When an ordinary plowboy is covered with the authority of God's Word, he becomes an extraordinary prophet! In Elisha's case, this authority was manifest in exactly twice the number of miracles that Elijah had performed, a genuine double portion of his mentor's anointing. The *tallit* as a mantle of anointing and authority had passed from the mentor to the student.

It is also possible that the profound power manifest in Elijah/Elisha's *tallit* was displayed in one additional event that occurred posthumously. When the dead body of a Moabite soldier was cast into Elisha's tomb, it came into contact with his bones and the *tallit* that enshrouded them. Immediately, the dead man was resurrected. Even in death either the prophet's remains or his *tallit* was still a channel for the manifestation of divine power.

In all subsequent generations, the term *passing the mantle* has come to mean the transfer of authority and anointing from one leader to another, from one generation to another. The *tallit* as the visible symbol of the Word of God is a demonstration of the positional and personal power that is transferred when "the mantle passes."

[1] 1 Kings 19:11-13.
[2] 1 Kings 19:15-18, NIV.
[3] 2 Kings 2:8.
[4] 2 Kings 2:1-6.
[5] 2 Kings 2:15.

Chapter 9

The Prayer Closet

The use of the *tallit* to separate oneself totally to communion with God was an institution in Judaism before the time of Jesus. This is perhaps the extended meaning of Jesus' recommendation concerning prayer in Matthew 6:6: ". . .when thou prayest, enter into thy closet, and when thou hast shut thy door, pray to thy father which is in secret. . ." The Greek word for closet is ταμεῖον (*tameion*), which means "an inner chamber, or a secret room." The closeting of oneself in the covering of the *tallit* was a symbolic separation from the world around the Jewish man. While the more ostentatious Pharisees made a show of their alms giving and their public prayers, the greater percentage of the Pharisees were sincere in their separating and secreting themselves in prayer so that with *kavanah* (proper attitude and concentration) they approached God and entered into a knowing relationship with him. While men in Jesus' time never covered their heads when praying as many modern Jews do, they did wrap themselves in their *tallit*, separating themselves unto God.

Prayer is not the chanting of a mantra in some mindless exercise that seeks to elevate one's consciousness and place him in contact with the "god within." It is not the "vain repetition"[1] *ad nauseum* of words and phrases, be they ever so lofty or inspiring. It is not reading, with mind detached, the words of a prayer book. It is not genuflection or self-flagellation. It is not the loud, public boastings of relationship with the Divine. Prayer is an intense, intimate, personal interaction between God and man. It is a dialogue in which one speaks to God and hears from God. It is a conversation that occurs only when man is intensely focused entirely on communion with God, having shut out all outside influences and distractions.

Rabbi Simeon in the *Mishnah's* tractate *Pirke Avot* 2:18 affirmed this truth: ". . . be scrupulous in reading the Shema and in prayer. When thou prayest, make not thy prayer a fixed form, but make it an entreaty and supplication of love before the Almighty. For the prophet Joel has said, 'Gracious and compassionate is he, long-suffering and abundant in mercy, and repenting of evil.'"[2]

When the Jew wraps himself in his praying mantle he excludes everything external so that his soul is consumed in thought about and in reverence toward God. He realizes that just as the *tallit* envelops his person, so his faith, to be effective, must involve the totality of his life. For him, therefore, there can be no dichotomy between the secular and the spiritual. Everything from the mundane to the sublime—the totality of life—is spiritual. Either God is manifest in every arena of life, or he is not manifest at all.

This is the kind of prayer life Jesus enjoined upon his disciples. Prayer, said the Master, is not a public display of vain repetitions, characterized by verbosity. Prayer is communication with God, and it is best manifest when one is focused on it by any means that can separate one from outside distractions. The Jewish man's *tallit* encloses him in a secret chamber, a prayer closet, shutting out the mundane, elevating his spirit into a knowing relationship with God.

It should also be noted that the prayer which Jesus instructed his disciples to pray was but a condensed version of various prayers employed in the synagogues of that day. It emphasized their relationship with God as Father, a long-standing tradition in Jewish worship, where God was addressed as *"Avinu, Malkeinu"* ("Our Father, Our King"). It honored the holiness and sovereignty of the one God. It asked, as all Jews do daily, for the emergence of the kingdom of God and for the manifestation of God's will in earth just as it is fulfilled in heaven. It petitioned God for necessary sustenance (so that one would not forsake God by being rich, nor dishonor God and himself by being placed in the position of having to steal bread[3]). It sought forgiveness of sins in the tradition of the Jews by first forgiving wrongs brought upon oneself by others. Then, it concluded with the petition for divine guidance, not into temptation, but into deliverance from evil. All of these affirmations and petitions were firmly rooted in the Jewish tradition of the *Tanakh* (Torah, Prophets, and Writings of the Hebrew Scriptures) and of the sages of Israel.

When one prays the prayers of God's Word in a condition of complete trust and concentration, he closets himself in the presence of God. For the Jews, this condition has been best reached by being covered with the praying mantle, the *tallit*. Since medieval times, some Jews have extended this practice to include the covering of the body, as well as the head, in complete separation unto God.

Whatever means one must use, he is constantly invited to the "secret place of the Most High" to enter into communion with the Almighty in an experience that transcends a mere logical, mental exercise and brings one into a visceral encounter with the Divine in which he can worship with all his heart, soul, mind, and strength.

: Matthew 6:7.

: Quoted in David deSola Pool. *Book of Prayers, According to the Custom of the Spanish and Portuguese Jews*. Second Edition (New York: Union of Sephardic Congregations. 1992). p. 241.

: Proverbs 30:8-9.

Chapter 10

A Blessing Covering

It is a tradition for blessings in Judaism to be performed under the *tallit*. The benedictions are Torah blessings; therefore. the *tallit* is a reminder that the power of God's Word blesses his people. Notable among these events are the blessing of children and the wedding ceremony.

When younger children receive the blessing of Jacob and the Aaronic benediction[1] they often stand under the *tallit*.[2] It is traditional after the *Shabbat* meal for the Jewish father to bless his children with the words of God recorded in Genesis 48:20. Numbers 6:24-26. and Isaiah 11:2. The father places his right hand on the head of each of his children and prays the following blessing: "May God make you like Ephraim and Manasseh [for sons] Rachel and Leah [for daughters]. The Lord bless you and keep you: the Lord make his face shine upon you and be gracious to you: the Lord turn his face toward you and give you peace. So they will put my name on the Israelites. and I will bless them. [At this point. the father may add a personalized blessing for his son or daughter.] May the Spirit of the Lord rest upon you–the Spirit of wisdom and understanding. the Spirit of counsel and of power. the Spirit of knowledge and of the fear of the Lord–

Jewish children being blessed
under the *tallit*

and may you delight in the fear of the Lord." Performing this blessing under the *tallit* reinforces for children the theme that God protects his people through the commandments of the Torah and through his provisions to bless the descendants of Israel always. A blessing is, in effect, a covering, an enshrouding of the one blessed in the providence of God. What better way to demonstrate this truth for children than by pronouncing God's blessing upon them under the covering of the *tallit*.

When a Jewish wedding takes place, the ceremony is generally performed under a *chuppah* (canopy), which is often comprised of a *tallit* held aloft by four men, especially in the Sephardic tradition.[3] (The Ashkenazi tradition often uses an embroidered cloth stretched over four wooden poles and set up under the open sky, preferably in a synagogue courtyard.) It is considered essential that this most important rite of passage in Jewish life be covered by the symbol of the Torah and of God's protection. The *chuppah* (canopy) of the *tallit* "represents the future home of the newly married roofed with sanctity."[4] Since the Torah is the source of the commandments that a man is to be joined to his wife and that husband and wife are to be fruitful and multiply, it is only proper that the one most visible symbol for the commandments of the Torah should be employed in the wedding itself. As a canopy it covers the bride and groom with the symbol of God's authority and of obedience to his commandments. It also symbolizes the divine protection of health and happiness of those who abide under the shadow of the Torah's marriage institution. Again, this is not just a mere talisman or amulet. It is a visible symbol of the very words of God.

Perhaps the precedent for wedding under the *chuppah* of a *tallit* was set at Sinai when Israel was espoused in marriage to God. The record declares that the holy mountain was enshrouded in clouds and smoke from the presence of the Almighty. Israel had been summoned from Egypt by the voice of God to appear before his mountain and receive the covenant of marriage that joined them in relationship with their God. And, indeed, the cloud and fire of his presence had accompanied them from the time of their exodus from Rameses until they came to Sinai. This covering with clouds as a symbol of divine protection can easily be seen in the expectation of God's covering presence both in marriage and in the blessing of children that he has ordained in his word.

This principle may also be seen in divorce, that painful process which sunders marriage. Divorce can be described as a rending of the covering garment of blessing upon a sanctified (or set apart) union. It may well be seen as a severing of the *tzitzit* of the *chupah's tallit*, removing the blessing of God's Torah upon the marriage and rendering it *pasul* or invalid. Just as ripping a *tzitzit* from one's *tallit* in biblical times represented a severing of authority, so a marriage is voided, its blessing severed through divorce. Because God hates divorce,[5] this is the reason for Jesus' injunction that man should not separate what God has joined together under his blessing.[6]

Both in the symbolism of blessing upon the constitution of marriage as being covered by the *tallit* and in the rending of the blessed state in divorce, one can see the importance of protecting and maintaining the covering of blessing, the enshrouding of God's provision for health and well being in marriage.Whatever is done in blessing through the provision of God's Word is an overshadowing of the wings of the Almighty, the covering of the Divine Presence that brings health and security.

[1] Genesis 48:20; Numbers 6:24-26.
[2] Efraim M. Rosenzweig. *We Jews* (New York: Hawthorn Books, Inc., 1977), p. 60.
[3] Alan Unterman, p. 151.
[4] W.O.E. Oesterly, p. 314.
[5] Malachi 2:16.
[6] Matthew 19:6, NIV.

Chapter 11

Your People, My People

She was recently widowed. A young woman full of vitality and hope, she found her plans and stability suddenly snatched away in terrible finality by the Grim Reaper. A stranger to all the promises of God, she had married into the family of Judah, the tribe to which God had promised rulership in Israel. She had great expectations for success in life, even though her family lived across the Jordan River from the Promised Land. Now she was faced with a terrible dilemma.

Ruth was a Moabitess, descended from Lot: Lot, who had chosen what appeared to be the best part of the land to which God had given Abraham title in one of the greatest real estate transactions of all time; Lot, who had ended up in history's most abominable city, Sodom, escaping by the skin of his teeth when God rained down fire and brimstone on that debauched, violent city; Lot, who had been tricked into a drunken stupor by his own daughters so that could conceive children by incest; Lot, the almost, but not quite Jew. One can readily see that Ruth the Moabitess had a less-than-distinguished birthright.

Death had been particularly cruel to Ruth's family. First her mother-in-law, Naomi, had become an untimely widow. Then, both of Naomi's sons had died, leaving Ruth and her sister-in-law as widows. Now it seemed time for this Moabitess girl to part company with Naomi and to distance herself from this string of misfortune. Naomi virtually insisted that she do so, trusting that perhaps she would find a husband among her own people. Despite the Levirate law among the Jews that required a brother to act as a surrogate father and produce children in his brother's name for his deceased brother's wife,[1] there was still no hope, for Naomi had no husband and no other sons and was likely too old to bear more.

Something profound had been stirring in Ruth's heart. Perhaps she had come to value her new identity as a part of the extended family of Israel. Whatever the reason, she simply could not bring herself to break her relationship with her mother-in-law. In an exclamation of ultimate devotion, she uttered those famous words that have echoed through the corridors of history: "Intreat me not to leave thee, or to return from following after thee: for whither thou goest, I will go; and where thou lodgest, I will lodge: thy people shall be my people, and thy God my God: where thou diest, will I die, and there will I be buried . . ."[2]

With these words and her subsequent actions, Ruth, the Gentile widow from Moab, proved that she was, in fact, a true daughter of Abraham, though not an actual descendant of the father of faith. She said and did what Abraham had done centuries before when he heard God's voice, saying, "Get up and go," and he immediately obeyed. He, too, had been a Gentile, a Babylonian by birth and a Syrian (Aramean) by nationality. He had left Ur of the Chaldees with his father, leaving his Gentile family, his occupation as an idol maker, and his religion of polytheism. He had found his progress toward God's goal for his life delayed in Haran of Syria when he heard that undeniable, penetrating voice, saying, "Go!" He then fully embraced El Shaddai and monotheism, crossed over the Euphrates, and began a new family, the Hebrews.

Now, Ruth made that same choice. She crossed over the Jordan River, abandoning her Gentile religion and embracing the religion of her mother-in-law. She became Jewish. With few expectations other than her new-found identity with God's chosen people, she left the land of her birth and entered the land of Judah.

When Naomi, with her daughter-in-law, reentered the land of promise, she was reintegrated with her family. It was there that she learned of a relative of wealth and honor in Bethlehem. His name was Boaz, and he was a man of great generosity. When he learned of Ruth, he insisted that during the time of harvest she glean only in his fields. Then he instructed his reapers to leave some of the wheat among the sheaves so that she could easily find it.

Perhaps in a preview of what was to occur in her life, Boaz pronounced this blessing upon Ruth: "The Lord recompense thy work, and a full reward be given thee of the Lord God of Israel, under whose wings thou art come to trust."[3] Boaz recognized that in embracing both the God and the people of Israel, Ruth had come to be included in God's covenant with Israel. She had placed herself wholly in the charge of God and his Torah. The word *wings* here is כָּנָף (*kanaph*), the corner of the *tallit* from which the *tzitziot* are appended. By embracing the Torah and all of its commandments, Ruth had placed herself under the wings of the Almighty and would be the beneficiary of his blessing and peace.

Naomi took pity upon the plight of her daughter-in-law when the time came for threshing the harvest, and she devised a plan by which she could claim the Levirate promise for her converted Gentile daughter-in-law. "Go in, uncover Boaz' feet, and lie down. He will tell you what to do," were the instructions from her mother-in-law that Ruth faithfully obeyed. When Boaz discovered her presence, she revealed her identity: "I am Ruth thine handmaid," and she implored him, "Spread therefore thy skirt over thine handmaid; for thou art a near kinsman."[4]

The next day Boaz redeemed Ruth as he sat among the elders at the city gate, pronouncing upon her the blessing that has been added to Jewish women and girls for all subsequent generations: "The Lord make [thee] like Rachel and Leah, which two did build the house of Israel." Then, in fulfillment of the law, Boaz married Ruth, who subsequently bore a son who was the grandfather of King David and a direct ancestor of Jesus, the Messiah.

This curious process of redemption and subsequent marriage began when Boaz covered Ruth with his "skirt." The word translated "skirt" is כָּנָף (*kanaph*), the word for the "corner" of the *tallit* where the *tzitzit* was located, not just the "skirt" or bottom edge of the mantle. This act of covering Ruth with the *tzitzit* of his *tallit* had powerful consequences. It meant that Boaz had accepted Ruth under his authority. There were no sensual overtones in this story, for both Ruth and Boaz were virtuous, as all the people of the city would attest. The *tzitzit* of the *tallit* represented the authority of the Torah commandments and the Word of God and was a mark of holiness and separation from the surrounding world. Boaz had merely recognized his own legal responsibilities toward this young widow and had made the gesture that she was covered by his integrity and by his determination to fulfill the Torah commandments which his *tzitzit* represented.

Can there be any doubt that the *tallit* and the *tzitzit* had profound significance even in the earliest times of Israel's covenantal relationship with God? This story should settle any questions. Boaz's *tallit* was in effect a *chuppah* of betrothal even before the details of the Levirate marriage could be worked out. Perhaps the *tzitzit* even reminded Boaz of his responsibility to bring up children in the name of his kinsman. When Obed was born to Ruth, the people said, "There is a son born to *Naomi.*"

The *tzitzit* of the *tallit*, then, had profound consequences for both Ruth and Naomi. Two widows, one of them a Gentile, who had been left alone were now fulfilled, brought into the house of one of Israel's wealthiest citizens, and inserted into the lineage of Israel's kings and its Messiah. And it all began to materialize when Boaz covered Ruth with the *tzitziyot* of his *tallit*.

---

[1] Deuteronomy 25:5-10.
[2] Ruth 1:16-17.
[3] Ruth 2:12.
[4] Ruth 3:9.

Chapter 12

God Is With You

A significant prophetic utterance involving the imagery of the *tzitzit* is found in Zechariah 8:23: "Thus saith the Lord of hosts; In those days it shall come to pass, that ten men shall take hold out of all languages of the nations, even shall take hold of the skirt of him that is a Jew, saying, We will go with you: for we have heard that God is with you." The word translated "skirt" is כָּנָף (*kanaph*), more accurately rendered "corner." This prophecy, then, predicts that ten men (representing a *minyan* or quorum of the Gentile nations of the world) will grasp the *tzitzit* at the corner of a Jew's *tallit*, declaring their intentions to follow him because they discern that God is with him. The question is, Who is this Jew and who are these Gentile men?

Zechariah's prophecy focuses on the historical rebuilding of the Temple in the days of Zerubbabel and Joshua. It speaks of God's blessing upon the restoration effort and declares that the nations will see his glory and be drawn into relationship with him. In the imagery of many other prophets, Zechariah envisioned the reestablishment of God's *menorah* light and the destruction of the "mountain" of opposition.[1] Daniel saw this as the kingdom of God hewn out of the mountains that destroyed the idolatrous kingdoms of man and initiated the everlasting dominion of God upon the earth.[2] Zechariah concluded his prophecy with the prediction that the Lord himself would come to stand upon the Mount of Olives,[3] vanquish the enemies of truth, and establish his kingdom on earth.

Zechariah's prophecy is filled with Messianic expectations and predictions of the One who is to come. He speaks of the manifestation of the One whose name is the BRANCH,[4] who will sit upon a throne as Priest and King. He speaks of the Messiah as a humble King who comes riding on a donkey,[5] devoid of arrogance and the usual pomp and circumstance that surrounds royalty. He predicts that the price of this Messiah would be thirty pieces of silver.[6] He speaks of a Son who would be pierced and for whom Israel would mourn.[7] But he also speaks of the Messiah's coming to bring universal peace, justice, and holiness.[8] With all the profound emphases upon Messianic expectations in Zechariah's visions and prophecies, it is very much in context to expect that the prediction of Zechariah 8:23 is also a Messianic prophecy.

When we view in this context Zechariah's prophecy of the ten Gentiles who grasp the *tzitzit* of the Jew's *tallit*, we can readily see the fulfillment in Jesus, the Jew who brought Israel's light to the nations of the Gentiles. Isaiah saw the Messiah in this same context: "It is a light thing that thou shouldest be my servant to raise up the tribes of Jacob, and to restore the preserved of Israel: I will also give thee for a light to the Gentiles, that thou mayest be my salvation unto the end of the earth."[9] Jesus was the light who extended salvation to the Gentiles, even to the ends of the earth. Two thousand years of history validate the fact that God's salvation, which was first manifest in the Abrahamic covenant's justification by faith and then in Judaism's ethical monotheism and the immutable moral law of God, has been taken to the Gentile nations. The central premises of the Hebraic faith of the Torah (albeit in an often radically modified and sometimes degenerate form) have been extended to the nations predominantly by the Christian church. In most cases, a syncretism or blending with the traditions, religions, and practices of the nations to which this redemptive message was preached has characterized Christian faith; however, the principles of God's eternal law have permeated much of world society through the church's missionary efforts, a tradition adopted from the proselytizing efforts of the Pharisees and pioneered in the church by Paul, the Pharisee.

From its inception, Christian faith was designed by Jesus and his apostles to be nothing more than a reformed Judaism. It was one of the many Judaisms in the first century, a Judaism that recognized in Jesus the fulfillment of Israel's Messianic expectations and discerned in him the completion of all the predictions of the *Tanakh* ("Old" Testament) regarding a suffering Messiah and its teachings on vicarious atonement and substitutionary righteousness. The earliest members of this movement were very much like their Jewish Lord, zealous for the Torah and meticulous in the application of its *halachah* (manner of walking or living) to their personal and corporate lives.[10] There was no attempt on the part of Jesus or his apostles to break away from the faith of their fathers and start a new religion. They merely sought to make their interpretation of the Torah and its fulfillment in Jesus normative for Jewish society. Jesus insisted that he did not come to destroy Judaism but to complete it.[11] Paul, the apostle

who was most instrumental in taking Israel's Messianic light to the nations, never wavered from his identity. "I am a Pharisee,"[12] he declared, affirming in the
holy temple that he had been faithful to the Torah and
to the traditions of his fathers.[13]

It was only through the error of subsequent centuries that Christianity was wrenched from its Hebraic
moorings, set adrift on a tide of syncretism and com-
promise with the traditions of the nations into which it
was carried, and propelled into the maelstrom of Hel-
lenic philosophy and Latin systems that finally severed its Jewish connection. These events precipitated
the great proto-schism that produced an ever-widen-
ing chasm between Christianity and its sister faith, rabbinic Judaism. But, the fact remains: Christianity is a
form of Judaism. However perverted it may have become from the inherent Jewish ideals of its founders,
Christianity without the core of faith that it received
from a Jewish Lord through a Jewish Book would be
no religion at all. All that is authentic in Christian faith
and experience is a direct product of the biblical Judaism through which Jesus and the apostles lived and
expressed their devotion to God.

Jesus was, indeed, the One who opened Abraham's
covenant to the entire world when he commissioned
his disciples: "Go ye into all the world, and preach the
gospel to every creature."[14] The good news that had
first been preached to Abraham[15] and then to all of
Israel[16] was then extended to all the world, to "every
creature." Jesus declared that the Holy Spirit which
was to come upon them would give them a new uniform as messengers of the kingdom of God which was
already breaking forth and that they would be witnesses beginning in Jerusalem and continuing to "the

uttermost part of the earth."[17]

Zechariah's prophecy, then, has been fulfilled in Jesus. He is the Jew whom the nations of the world have followed because they have recognized that God is with him–indeed, in him. The Gentile peoples, represented by the ten men, have laid hold on the *tzitzit* of Jesus' *tallit*, recognizing, as the infirm woman did, the authority in the "hem of his garment." Just as the *tzitzit* in Bible days symbolized the authority of its wearer and the power of the Torah commandments of God to bring health and prosperity to those who observe them, so the Name (authority) of Jesus has brought deliverance from superstition and evil to millions of Gentiles around the world, bringing to them a "perfect law of freedom."

What the written Torah has done for ancient Israel and for all Jews of subsequent generations, the living, incarnate Torah has done for multiplied millions of Christian believers around the world and across twenty centuries. Through Jesus, Gentiles of every nation under heaven have been grafted into Israel's family tree of salvation, where they have drawn from the rich sap both from the tap root (Jesus) and from the entire root system of the Torah, the prophets, and the sages of Israel. They have been converted to the reformed Judaism that Jesus brought to the nascent church. Those who have grasped his "coattails" have been drawn by Jesus into realms of glory and relationship with the Eternal Father that were impossible in their former pagan cultures. They have actually become seated with him in heavenly places at the Father's right hand.[18]

Unfortunately, Gentile believers in Jesus as the Messiah have only remotely recognized his Jewishness,

if at all. Most of them have viewed him as the cosmic
Christ and have not understood his intimate connection with the People of the Book, his Jewish brethren.
Both historically and in the age come, however, Jesus
is a Jew.

A profound restoration movement is occurring in-
ternationally as the society of man enters a new millennium. The Hebraic foundations of Christian faith
are being restored in a move of the Holy Spirit that is
transcending nationalism, ethnicity, and denomination-
alism. Increasing numbers of Christians are reconnect-
ing with the Judaic heritage of their faith. They are
understanding as never before the deep meaning in the
teachings of Jesus and the apostles as they place them
back into the context of the Hebraic matrix from which
they emerged. People from all nations are grasping the
tzitzit of Jesus' *tallit*, touching the "hem of his garment" and finding that, indeed, God is present. And
they are resolved to follow him into full and complete
relationship with the God of the Bible, fully experienc-
ing the salvation that is "from the Jews," worshipping
the Father in spirit and in truth.[19]

For many, laying hold on Jesus' *tzitzit* is understanding the Jewishness of this Yeshua of Nazareth. It
is an affirmation that "we will go with *you*," the Jewish Messiah, and not merely with the Gentilized Christ
of antinomian, anti-Semitic Christian tradition. It is a
commitment to be healed from the anemia of non-
biblical beliefs and be restored to the full health of
biblically Hebraic faith. Like Ezra of old, these believers have purposed to walk with God by studying his
Word, practicing its precepts, and teaching God's ways
to others.[20] They are laying hold on the Torah (symbolized by the *tzitzit*), claiming it as the church's heri-

tage, the God-breathed Holy Scripture that is profitable for teaching and equipping every man and woman of God for the good works that will bring glory to the heavenly Father.[21]

In the final analysis, by the end of the age billions of Gentile men and women will have taken hold of the *tzitzit* of the One who is a Jew, embracing his ancient faith and following the Lamb wherever he goes.[22]

[1] Zechariah 4:7.
[2] Daniel 2:44-45.
[3] Zechariah 14:4.
[4] Zechariah 3:8.
[5] Zechariah 9:9.
[6] Zechariah 11:12.
[7] Zechariah 12:10; 13:6.
[8] Zechariah 14:1-21.
[9] Isaiah 49:6.
[10] Acts 21:20; 22:3.
[11] Matthew 5:17-19.
[12] Acts 23:6.
[13] Acts 21:24; Galatians 1:14.
[14] Mark 16:15.
[15] Galatians 3:8.
[16] Hebrews 4:2.
[17] Acts 1:8.
[18] Ephesians 2:6.
[19] John 4:23; cf. 2 Corinthians 5:2; Matthew 11:12.
[20] Ezra 7:10.
[21] 2 Timothy 3:16; Matthew 5:16.
[22] Revelation 14:4, NIV.

Chapter 13

Healing
Wings

One of the most evocative and powerful of all
Messianic prophecies is found in Malachi 4:2: "But
unto you that fear my name shall the Sun of righteousness arise with healing in his wings. . ." This prophecy speaks of the person and work of the Messiah at
his coming. It reveals much to us about the very nature of the Messiah, but it also helps us to understand
the profound accomplishment of the Messianic Age.

Messianism is at the very heart of all biblical religion. Both Judaism and Christianity, in the words of
Martin Buber, share "a book and an expectation." The
first promise of the Scriptures is a Messianic prophecy: "He [the Messiah] shall bruise thy head."[1] The
very last promise of the Bible is also a Messianic promise: "Surely I come quickly."[2] From beginning to end,
the very fabric of both the Hebrew Scriptures and the
Apostolic Writings is woven around the scarlet thread
of Messianic expectation.

It is for this reason that Christian faith is inherently Messiah-centered, Christocentric. While Jesus
lived a Torahcentric lifestyle, the hallmark of Christian
faith is Christocentricity. "Whatsoever ye do in word
or deed, do all in the name of the Lord Jesus, giving
thanks to God and the Father by him," the apostle

declared.[3] Christian faith is not Torahcentric, bibliocentric, or ecclesiocentric. It is not focused in any denomination or in any human personality. It is Messiahcentric, focused in the person of the Messiah, Yeshua. The Messianic expectation has, and is, and will ever remain the church's "blessed hope."[4]

The word *Messiah* is a transliteration of the Hebrew מָשִׁיחַ (*Mashiach*), which literally means "smeared with oil." When New Testament writers were seeking a Greek word to translate their native Hebrew, they chose Χριστός (*Christos*), a term that referred to the smearing of oil, covering the bodies of athletes in ancient Olympic tradition. The Greek term has come into English as "Christ."

Mashiach is the constant promise of the Hebrew Scriptures. Balaam saw him as "a star" rising "out of Jacob."[5] David saw him as his Lord who sat at the right hand of Y/H/W/H to whom he would "give the uttermost part of the earth for [*an*] habitation."[6] Micah predicted his place of birth and spoke of his eternal preexistence.[7] Isaiah spoke of the birth of one who would be called, "Wonderful Counselor, Mighty God, Everlasting Father, Prince of Peace," and then spoke of his death as a vicarious atonement for the sins of all: "He was wounded for our transgressions . . . and with his stripes we are healed."[8] David spoke of his resurrection: "For thou wilt not leave my soul in hell; neither wilt thou suffer thine Holy One to see corruption."[9] Malachi predicted his coming as a "great and dreadful day of the Lord," but also as a time of healing.[10]

Malachi's prophecy first speaks specifically of those for whom the Messiah will arise: ". . .you that fear my name. . ." This reference to those who revere

and honor God and his Word (the Torah) is clarified in
Ezra 10:3: " . . . those that tremble at the commandment of our God." These are the הַרֵדִים (*haredim*),
the righteous ones who believe God's Word and do it,
including even Gentiles, the "God-fearers" of the first
century. In the climactic event of history when "all the
proud . . . and all that do wickedly shall be stubble:
and the day that cometh shall burn them up,"[11] these
haredim, both Jews and Gentiles, will stand with the
Messiah upon Mount Zion as he establishes peace upon
earth to men of good will.

The metaphor that is used in Malachi 4 for the
Messiah is unique to this passage and evokes powerful
imagery. The coming one is the "Sun of righteousness." The most frequent biblical metaphor describing
God is fire. "Our God is a consuming fire,"[12] the Scriptures tell us. No more clear example of this could be
cited than the *Shekhinah* which appeared over the camp
of Israel, on the blackened summit of Sinai, and on
the mercy seat of the ark of the covenant in the Most
Holy Place of the tabernacle in the wilderness, or the
cloven tongues of fire on the believers on the day of
Pentecost in Acts 2.

The glory of the coming Messiah was of such
magnitude that the only thing to which the prophet
could compare it was the light of the sun. Others used
the same idea, with different terms: Peter called Jesus
the "Day Star"[13]; John saw him as the "Bright Morning Star."[14] The brightness of the Messiah is, in fact,
the light that makes all other light pale in comparison.
He is the light that existed with[15] and emanated from
the presence of God from before creation.[16] He is the
Eternal Word (*Memra*, *Logos*) of God,[17] encapsulated
in the Torah, incarnated in the person of Jesus of Naza-

reth. He is Torah incarnate.

The *Logos*/Christ/Messiah is that light that was brought forth at the moment when God first spoke his Word: "Let there be light." This is the light that existed for three of creation's days before the sun, moon, and stars were created. In the statement, "God saw the light that it was good," the phrase *the light* in Hebrew is אֶת־הָאוֹר (*et ha-or*). When the numerical equivalents of the letters in this phrase are totaled, the sum is 613, the precise number of commandments in the Torah. The Torah is the Word of God that enlightens the eyes of man. It is the light that was with God from the beginning of creation, the Word of God.

That Word, however, is both the written record of God's sayings to man and the person of the *Logos* who was incarnated in Jesus. Jesus, then, is the light who eternally reveals the heavenly Father. "For God, who commanded the light to shine out of darkness, hath shined in our hearts, to give the light of the knowledge of the glory of God in the face of Jesus Christ."[18] Jesus was, indeed, correct when he declared: "I am the light of the world."[19] He is the light that lightens every man, just as much as the light of the sun makes natural vision possible. He is God's lamp and man's light, the living Menorah, because he is the life in the *Logos*. Indeed, Jesus is the Sun of righteousness, who, in his Triumphal Entry into Jerusalem, came from the east, the Mount of Olives, and entered the city's Eastern Gate. Like the sun, he will again arise upon that Holy City from the east as his feet stand on the Mount of Olives and he enters the city through its now-sealed Eastern Gate.

Malachi's prophecy speaks of the Messiah as being the Sun of "righteousness." This is to say that he is the radiance of justice and rightness. Uniquely and as no other person who has ever lived upon the face of planet earth, Jesus of Nazareth embodied the righteousness of God. It was said of him that he knew no sin, neither was deceit found in his mouth.[20] He was the first and only person who established perfect personal righteousness by complete observance of every precept of the Torah. "I have kept my Father's commandments," he attested.[21] When the time came for his death upon the cross, he could confidently declare, "The prince of this world cometh, but he hath nothing in me."[22]

Though hosts of dedicated, pious men and women in Israel had sought diligently to establish righteousness by faith in, and obedience to, God's commandments,[23] all had failed and come short of the glory of God.[24] Many contemporaries of Jesus were so devoted to establishing their own righteousness that they failed to see and partake of the righteousness of God in the person of Jesus.[25] God made Jesus to be righteousness for everyone who believes in his heart that God raised him from the dead.[26] The righteousness of Jesus is imputed to the believer for his faith[27] so that the believer also is clothed in the righteousness of God,[28] a righteousness that exceeds even the righteousness of the Pharisees (*Perushim*, righteous ones).[29] As by the sin of Adam, the corporate head of the human race, sin and death came into the world, so by the righteousness of the second Adam, eternal life came to all as the free gift of God that brought all men unto the justification of perfect righteousness.[30]

Jesus was, indeed, the Sun of righteousness, the express image of the person of the Father.[31] When he returns, he will restore perfect justice and rectitude to the earth so that Jerusalem, the capital city of world government, will be called the "city of righteousness"[32] and the righteousness thereof will go forth as a lamp that will enlighten the earth and bring the nations into the righteousness of God.[33]

When this Sun of righteousness comes, he will bring with him healing. The Hebrew word translated "healing" in Malachi 4:2 is מַרְפֵּא (*marpe*) from the root רָף (*raph*), a Hebrew onomatopoeia that images the action by the sound of the word. It means to repair in the sense of sewing together a torn garment with a needle and thread. One can hear the action of the needle passing through the fabric with the spoken word, *raph*.[34] This root word is also used as one of the titles of the Divine: *Y-H-W-H Rophe*, "Eternal Healer."[35] It speaks of restoration: "to recover what is stolen, to restore to pristine felicity, and, when used in the *pi'el*, to mend or repair a broken altar."[36]

The healing that the Messiah brings is more far reaching than a miraculous, instantaneous physical recovery from some physical or psychological malady. And, no doubt, the healing of diseases which were wrought through the ministry of Jesus was one of the signs of his Messiahship and a fulfillment of this prophecy. The more far-reaching consequence of this "healing," however, is the restoration of planet Earth to the state of the Garden of Eden, again a Jewish expectation. What has been broken by the greed and violence of men will be mended by the hand of the Messiah. The earth will experience a global restoration, ecologically, economically, politically, and religiously when Yeshua HaMashiach returns to this planet. What "all the king's horses and all the king's men" with their massive programs of social and political activism cannot put together again will be fully restored when the Messiah comes.

The healing, מַרְפֵּא (*marpe*), that Messiah brings to mankind is שָׁלוֹם (*shalom*), universal peace. It is peace in the sense of an absence of conflict, but it is more: it is wholeness, completeness, health. Indeed, *shalom* comes from the Hebrew root שׁלם (*sh-l-m*), which means restoration. The coming of the שַׂר שָׁלוֹם (*Sar Shalom*), the Prince of Peace, is to be a massive restoration, returning the earth and all its ecosystems, its economy, its socio-political structure, and its religion to health and wholeness. This is the promise of the Messiah's coming: "And he shall send Jesus Christ . . . in the time of the restoration of all things the prophets have declared."[37] It is no coincidence that this restoration of planet earth and all its inhabitants to the health of *shalom* will be at the hand of Yeshua, whose very name יֵשׁוּעַ (*Yeshua*) corresponds to the Hebrew word יְשׁוּעָה (*yeshuah*), translated "health [of my countenance]" in Psalm 43:5, but more accurately meaning, "rescue, salvation."

Malachi informs us that the restoration that the Messiah brings will be "in his wings." The Hebrew word for "wings" here is כָּנָף (*kanaph*), the same word for the "corner" of the garment, the word David used in describing the trust of God's people in the shadow of his wings.[38] The Messiah will not descend from heaven, flapping fine-feathered wings. He will descend wearing a vesture similar to that which he wore in his Judaean experience, the *tallit*, with its four *tzitziyot* hanging from its corners (wings). This garment, along with his grooming, immediately identified Jesus as a Jew to the Samaritan woman in John 4. It will again identify him as the Jew of Jews when he returns in power and great glory. As his *tallit* and its flowing *tzitziyot* are spread out by his outstretched arms of blessing to his people and of judgment to the enemies of truth, every eye shall see him and the healing in his wings.

The Apocalypse paints this vivid picture of the *parousia* of our Lord: "I saw heaven opened, and behold a white horse; and he that sat upon him was called Faithful and True . . . and his name is called The Word of God . . . and he hath on his vesture and on his thigh a name written, KING OF KINGS, AND LORD OF LORDS."[39] The Messiah who comes to establish God's dominion upon the earth in an age of peace is called "The Word of God," a name that is written on his vesture (טַלִּית, *tallit*) and upon his thigh as "King of kings, and Lord of lords." Could it be that what will appear on the Messiah's thigh will actually be the *tzitziyot*, which for millennia have symbolized the very Word of God, the Torah? We cannot be sure; however, we may be certain that the returning Messiah (or the coming Messiah of Jewish expectation) will be wearing a *tallit* (vesture) that will have *tzitziot* appended to its four corners.

This may well be the reason for the apocalyptic description not only of Jesus, but also of the armies of heaven that return with him at his coming as all being "clothed in white linen" (the *sadiyn* or fine linen *tallit*). The Messiah who departed the earth wrapped in fine linen will return again so clothed, clearly recognizable as the *Jewish* Messiah by his grooming and garments, and the armies with him will also be so distinguished by their fine linen *tallitot*.

We more fully understand the imagery in this, the focal point of the Apocalypse, when we remember that Jesus was a Jew and that his religion was Judaism. He was Torah observant, keeping all the commandments, as he, himself, affirmed in John 15:20. His dress and grooming were, therefore, Jewish. He lived a Jew,[40] died a Jew,[41] resurrected a Jew,[42] ascended a Jew,[43] and will return again a Jew.[44] When he returns, he will look as he did when he left: he will be recognizable from his outward appearance as a Jew. His *tallit*, complete with *tzitziot*, will demonstrate his authority to bring restoration to earth by the power that is demonstrated in the corners of his *tallit*, the visible symbol of the Torah, God's Word.

Is it any wonder, then, that the Jewish people of Jesus' day who "trusted that it had been he which should have redeemed Israel"[45] would have expected this Messiah to have healing in his wings, in the *tzitzit* on the corners of his *tallit*? Would it not be expected that all who had this Messianic expectation would have touched "the hem of his garment" and have been healed of their diseases, restored to health and vitality? With a renewed understanding of the importance of *tallit* and *tzitzit* in first-century Jewish tradition, we can readily understand those Israelites' desire to "touch the hem of his garment" and be impacted by the power of the Word of God which promised them that God "healeth all thy diseases."[46]

The Sun of righteousness will return to this planet to manifest the healing power first demonstrated in the hem of his garment. In the authority revealed in the *tzitziot* of his *tallit*, he will enshroud all of humanity in the *Shekhinah*, the eternal presence and glory of God. All that was lost through Adam's fall will be fully restored through Messiah's victory. The earth will be renewed as the Garden of Eden, and there will be universal peace in Messiah's Restoration Millennium.

[1] Genesis 3:15.
[2] Revelation 22:20.
[3] Colossians 3:17.
[4] Titus 2:13.
[5] Numbers 24:17.
[6] Psalm 2.
[7] Micah 5:2.
[8] Isaiah 9:6-7; 53:1-12.
[9] Psalm 16:10.
[10] Malachi 4:2, 5.
[11] Malachi 4:1.
[12] Deuteronomy 4:24; Hebrews 12:29.
[13] 1 Peter 1:19.
[14] Revelation 22:16.
[15] 1 Timothy 6:16.
[16] Hebrews 1:1-2.
[17] John 1:1-4.
[18] 2 Corinthians 4:6.
[19] John 8:12.
[20] 1 Peter 2:22.
[21] John 15:10.
[22] John 14:30.
[23] Romans 10:3.
[24] Romans 3:23.
[25] Romans 10:3, 4.
[26] Romans 10:9.
[27] Romans 4:5, 22.
[28] Ephesians 6:14.
[29] Matthew 5:20.
[30] Romans 5:18.
[31] Hebrews 1:1, 2.
[32] Isaiah 1:26.
[33] Isaiah 61:11; 62:1.
[34] H.W.F. Gesenius. *Gesenius' Hebrew-Chaldee Lexicon to the Old Testament* (Grand Rapids: Baker Books, 1979), p. 775.
[35] Exodus 15:26.
[36] H.W.F. Gesenius. *Gesenius' Hebrew-Chaldee Lexicon to the Old Testament*, p. 775.
[37] Acts 3:20-21, literal translation.
[38] Psalm 36:7.
[39] Revelation 19:11, 13, 16.
[40] Romans 9:4-5; Hebrews 7:14.
[41] Matthew 27:37.
[42] Luke 24:44-46.
[43] Acts 2:30-31.
[44] Acts 1:8-11.
[45] Luke 24:21.
[46] Psalm 103:3.

Chapter 14

Being
Clothed Upon

Wrapped in the white *tallit* symbolizing the righteousness of the Holy One, the Jewish people are visible reminders of the force for justice and honor in the world. The fact that the *tallit* represents a uniform that marks the Jewish man as a part of God's army of righteous ones who seek to spread the Word of his commandments is rich with symbolism that speaks of spiritual vestment that far transcends the outward material demonstration.

For the Christian, the *tallit* visibly and dramatically underscores the believer's need to be clothed upon with the Holy Spirit and his empowering grace. Jesus commanded his disciples to "tarry in Jerusalem until ye be endued with power from on high."[1] For the first century Jewish believer in Jesus, his commandment to be endued (clothed) with power would have instantly invoked the powerful imagery of the *tallit*, with its flowing *tzitziyot*, for the outer garment of their day was the *tallit*. Any garment with which they were to be clothed would have been seen as a *tallit*. Jesus was promising to enrobe the believers in the vestment of the Holy Spirit, himself. And, indeed, while they were fervently engaged in morning prayers on the day of Pentecost, the disciples were clothed in a new spiritual uniform of power that transcended the material uniform which demonstrated the Torah.[2] Their new *tallit* was the very Lawgiver himself, indwelling the lives of the believers and empowering them to fulfill the Torah in a new and living way. They were now arrayed in the finest linen, the light and splendor of the Holy Spirit.

For the believer today, this is an important paradigm of power. The Holy Spirit with which one is clothed manifests a uniform which sets him apart and endows him with authority far beyond his human capacity. Without the uniform of the Spirit, every man is serpent's meat, vulnerable to the beguiling devices of the one who orchestrated the fall of his grandfather Adam.[3] The *tallit* underscored to the Israelites the commandments of God essential to their existence as individuals and as a people and identified them to others as a people chosen and sanctified unto God. In the same way, the Holy Spirit affirms that the believer can do all things through the Spirit of the Messiah's strength,[4] and it identifies him on sight to the demonic world as possessing a power superior to its devices. Just as the *tallit* with its trailing *tzitiyot* was an image of dedication to God, so the Holy Spirit clothes the believer with the power to walk with God without condemnation.[5]

The Scriptures promise that the believer who has been endued with the Holy Spirit possesses the same power which produced the resurrection of Jesus.[6] This same imagery of enduement is clearly demonstrated in the Jewish doctrine of resurrection, the exposition of which was attributed to the Pharisees in the time of Jesus and the apostles. Paul uses this metaphor in an extended discourse on the resurrection body which is prepared for every believer. "For while we are in this tent, we groan and are burdened, because we do not wish to be unclothed but to be clothed with our heavenly dwelling, so that what is mortal may be swallowed up by life."[7] Paul's reference to being clothed upon with a tent (tabernacle) strongly suggests the *tallit*, for the befringed vesture of the Jewish man in biblical times was also seen as a tent.

Interestingly enough, Paul's metaphor speaks not of an entirely future creation but of an already completed provision. "For we know that if our earthly house of this tabernacle were dissolved, we *have* a building of God, an house not made with hands, eternal in the heavens,"[8] the apostle declares. This tent of the resurrection body is already prepared and awaiting the time of the last shofar blast when the Spirit-clothed believer will be vested with his body which is from heaven.

The power that has been given him as the down payment on eternal life[9] will also clothe the believer in a body of light similar to the glorious body which Jesus received when the stone was rolled away from his tomb and he came forth triumphant in the blinding light of resurrection.[10] It will be as though the believer has been enshrouded in a new *tallit*, covered in a tent of perfection.

The apostle John also uses this same metaphor in describing the reward given to the overcomer: he "shall be clothed in white raiment."[11] He also described the innumerable multitude of those who are resurrected as being "clothed in white robes."[12] The Greek word for robe is *stolé* which denotes both the *tallit* and the Christian liturgical vestment which is derived from it. In the light of John's culture, whether it speaks figuratively of the resurrection body or literally of the vestures, the *stolé* of the redeemed could only be the *tallit*.

The armies of heaven which accompany the Messiah at his return in John's Revelation[13] are seen as being clothed in fine linen garments, clearly indicating the *tallit*, both figuratively (spiritually) and literally. Like the Messiah, the *tzitziyot* of whose *tallit* will rest upon his thigh announcing his name, The Word of God,[14] the redeemed armies of heaven will be clothed in dazzling white garments of righteousness, the *tallitot* with *tzitziyot* streaming from their corners announcing the Messianic Kingdom of justice and peace.

[1] Luke 24:49, NIV.
[2] Acts 2:1-4.
[3] 2 Corinthians 11:3.
[4] Philippians 4:13.
[5] Romans 8:1.
[6] Romans 8:11.
[7] 2 Corinthians 5:2-4, NIV.
[8] 2 Corinthians 5:1.
[9] 2 Corinthians 1:22.
[10] Philippians 3:21.
[11] Revelation 3:5.
[12] Revelation 6:11; 7:9.
[13] Revelation 19:14.
[14] Revelation 19:16.

Chapter 15

An Ensign for a Prayer Nation

Considering the predominance of secularists both in the Zionist movement and in the earliest stages of the restoration of a Jewish homeland, the design for the Israeli flag that has represented the State of Israel for more than fifty years is nothing less than extraordinary, perhaps evidence of divine providence.

There can be no doubt but that the hand of God was at work in divine sovereignty, orchestrating the circumstances which led to the United Nations' recognition of the statehood of Israel in 1948. What had never occurred in the annals of history was accomplished when an ancient people who had been forcefully displaced from their native land nearly two thousand years earlier were once again enfranchised with the right to self-determination in their own nation. The prediction that Isaiah had made over twenty-five hundred years before it was literally fulfilled when the nation was "born in a day"![1]

Amos had predicted that the time would come when the Jewish people would be planted in their own land, "never to be plucked out again."[2] It would have seemed to any logical thinker, however, that such a thing would be an impossibility. No people in history had been conquered and scattered across the face of the globe only to return and restore their national sovereignty after nearly two millennia. Indeed, most Jews had reconciled themselves to the reality that such a restoration could come only in the Messianic Age and had resigned themselves to make the best of their situation by assimilating into the political processes of the nations in which they had been dispersed.

Then, at the end of the nineteenth century, spontaneously and with little realistic expectations, the Zionist movement was birthed. Men of unusual passion arose to insist that both the nation of Israel and the Hebrew language were to be restored so that the Jewish people could have a measure of self-determination and security. Over the subsequent decades, the movement was nurtured by men of vision and passion, including Theodor Herzl, who championed the cause before governing authorities in the western nations. The recognition that the movement received with the Balfour Declaration only twenty years later was amazing, despite the fact that early ideas called for establishing a Jewish state in Uganda rather than in the land of Jewish ancestors.

In the 1930's anti-Semitism reared its ugly head in Germany in the form of the Nazi party and its leader, the megalomaniacal Adolph Hitler, who found an easy scapegoat for German economic conditions in its Jewish population. As Europe was plunged into World War II by the expansionist attacks of the German blitzkrieg, Hitler and his henchmen escalated their overt anti-Semitism, proposing a "final solution" to the "Jewish problem," nothing less than a mass-extermination of Jewish men, women, and children which, if successful, would have resulted in genocide.

Thus began the *Shoah*. Systematically and unrelentingly, Jews were arrested throughout Europe wherever the Third Reich gained ascendancy. First, they were executed and buried in mass graves. Later, a more efficient killing system was devised. Jews were herded into railroad cattle cars and transported to specially prepared death camps. They were brought into gas chambers that were disguised as showers, and lethal cyanide gas was introduced, killing all the occupants. Then, after their corpses had been desecrated, removing anything of value, including in some cases even their skin, they were reduced to ashes in the crematoria that sent up the smoke of the Holocaust in which six million Jews were killed, including more than one million children.

When the war concluded and the Allied forces discovered the full nature of history's most grotesque and concentrated atrocity against any people group, the corporate conscience of the world was pricked by the plight of the Jews. Part of this guilt resulted from the fact that the Allied nations shared complicity in the slaughter of the Jews by not allowing early Jewish immigration into their nations and then by not intervening when they had gained knowledge of the concentration camps and the systematic slaughter that was being carried out there.

Finally, the United Nations recognized the Jewish people's right to self-determination in establishing their own state in the land of their ancestors. On May 14, 1948, the leaders of the new Israel declared its official constitution. Thus was the nation of Israel restored after nearly two millennia of nonexistence. Its formation and recognition by the United Nations was a miracle; however, its survival in its earliest years was a greater miracle as Israeli patriots defended the nation despite being vastly outnumbered.

In October of 1948, the Provisional Council of the State of Israel adopted the blue and white colors with the Shield of David as the flag of Israel. This flag was unfurled on May 11, 1949, at Lake Success in New York when Israel became the fifty-ninth member of the United Nations. It has flown over the nation for more than fifty years now, a testimony to the sovereignty and faithfulness of God in bringing to pass his prophetic promises to his chosen people.

The design of the Israeli flag is the same as that of the Zionist flag that was used at the First Zionist Congress in Basel, Switzerland, in 1897. David Wolfsohn, the distinguished Zionist leader who succeeded Theodor Herzl as president of the World Zionist Organization in 1905, was instrumental in working out this design. Here is Wolfsohn's own account of the development of the Zionist flag which became the Israeli flag:

At the behest of our leader Herzl, I came to Basle to make preparations for the Zionist congress, to assure its success and to avoid any opening for detractors. Among the many problems that occupied me then was one which contained something of the essence of the Jewish problem: What flag would we hang in the Congress Hall? . . . Then an idea struck me. We have a flag—and it is blue and white. The *tallit* (prayer-shawl) which we wrap ourselves when we pray: that is our symbol. Let us take this *tallit* from its bag and unroll it before the eyes of Israel and the eyes of all nations. So I ordered a blue and white flag with the Shield of David painted upon it. That is how our national flag, that flew over Congress Hall, came into being. And no one expressed any surprise or asked whence it came, or how.[3]

Amazing? Yes! Apropos? To be sure! It doubtless was a stroke of divine providence that the nation which God originally chose to be a kingdom of priests should, in its restoration, be represented by a flag patterned after one of observant Judaism's most clear symbols of subjection to divine guidance and protection, the *tallit*. God predicted that the temple of his people would be a "house of prayer for all people." Israel is to be a praying nation. It is altogether appropriate, then, that the symbol of this nation should be patterned after the prayer shawl in which observant Jews wrap themselves for morning prayers.

Perhaps divine providence gained ascendancy over secularist, agnostic Jews who established the initially socialist government in Israel. The flag that has flown over the state of Israel for more than fifty years has been a symbol of prayer, even though many officials have been neither Torah observant nor devoted to prayer. Just as the individual Jew covers himself in the *tallit* as a symbol of his being enshrouded in the Torah and thereby in God, himself, so the nation, whether wittingly or not, is covered with the same symbol of blessing and divine protection.

The Israeli flag may well even be a material reflection of the spiritual statement which King David made to Israel: "Thou hast given a banner to them that fear thee, that it may be displayed because of the truth."[4] Being patterned after the *tallit*, it certainly is designed after an object which represents and displays truth (the Torah) to Jews around the world. It also represents

God's sovereign action in ensuring that the banner that is unfurled over the restored nation of Israel should demonstrate his intentions to overshadow his people with his wings, using his Torah as a guardian for them until the advent of the Messianic Age.

[1] Isaiah 66:8, NIV.
[2] Amos 9:11-15.
[3] Quoted in "The Flag of Israel," a brochure produced and distributed by the Information Department of the Embassy of Israel in Washington, D.C.
[4] Psalm 60:4.

Chapter 16

A Rich
Tradition

The wearing of *tzitziyot* or tassels attached to the four corners of the outer garment (whether the ancient mantle or the more modern prayer shawl) is a rich tradition of devotion to the specific details of a divine commandment. Jews of every generation who have sought to fulfill this commandment have done so because of the divine initiative some four millennia ago which brought our father Abraham into relationship with El Shaddai and because of God's summons of their ancestors to Sinai to enter into covenantal relationship with him. One must remember that this practice is the result of divine imperative, not man's invention: it was God's commandment to his people, not their scheme to secure or maintain his attention.

The *tallit* is a memory device of divine design that for centuries has served the function of demanding each descendant of the Sinai *Kahal* or congregation (*Qehillah* in modern Hebrew) to "remember all of the commandments of the Lord and do them."

For those who know nothing of the biblical basis for the *tallit* and *tzitzit* and for the Jewish literalist interpretation of the commandment and tradition which surrounds its continuing use, the practice may seem quaint and anachronistic. Indeed, many modern Jews regard the *tallit* tradition in this manner. For those who make it a part of their daily devotion to God and his Word, however, it is rich in meaning.

Some have suggested that the *tallit* represents nothing more than a talisman, a superstitious effort to contact the Divine. Theodor Reik has proposed that the *tallit* is really a woolen surplice intended to complement the leather *tefillin* as a "quasi-shamanistic attempt on the part of the Jew to dress up like his ancient totem animal."[1] The reference is to the statues of the golden calf that were erected by Aaron at Sinai and by Jeroboam at the Beth El sanctuary. We must remember, however, that both of these instances occurred in times of rebellion against the true worship of God and were judged as such with profound consequences. Though many of the Israelites frequently involved themselves in the pagan rituals employed in worship of the tribal deities of their neighbors, there is no evidence that Israel worshipped God through totemistic symbols of a sacred beast.[2] Reik's suggestion would be correct if he had simply noted that the Jewish people's wrapping themselves in *tallit* both in ancient times and today has been an act of *imitatio Dei*, for this act of remembrance of all the com-

—Jewish Father and Son
in their *Tallitot*

mandments of the Eternal is the ultimate act of submission to the divine will expressed in the Torah and represents an effort to be like God. Just as God shelters all who believe on him under the wings of his divine protection, so the Jews are covered by the winged corners of the garment that manifests Torah to them.

For the Jew in life and in death, the *tallit* is a symbol of the equality of man. A Chassidic saying has it that "when two Jews associate on an equal footing and discuss a subject of Torah, the indwelling presence of God is with them. But when one of them holds himself superior to the other, God is not there."[3] Judaism was the first grand experiment in the democratization of religion. To the Jew, every human being is a "child of God," born equal, distinguished only by virtue. This is why all Jews "conceal the superficiality and diversity of their everyday clothing, covering them[selves] with the identical tallit."[24] Even in death, there is no ostentatious display for the rich. Every Jewish man is interred in simple white clothing and his own *tallit*. Indeed, the *tallit* may well have been the fine linen shroud or the "napkin" used in the interment of Jesus.

Before putting on the four-cornered garment, Jewish men for some nineteen centuries have recited the following benediction: "Blessed art thou, O Lord, our God, King of the universe, who has sanctified us by thy commandments, and has commanded us to wrap

בָּרוּךְ אַתָּה יי אֱלֹהֵינוּ מֶלֶךְ הָעוֹלָם אֲשֶׁר קִדְּשָׁנוּ בְּמִצְוֹתָיו וְצִוָּנוּ לְהִתְעַטֵּף בַּצִּיצִת:

—Blessing recited when preparing to wrap oneself in *Tallit* ourselves in the *tzitzit*." While it is believed that this benediction dates to the Tannaic period after the destruction of the Temple, it is possible that Jesus recited some form of it. Today, this same benediction is embroidered on the *atarah* (crown) of most prayer shawls so that a man may see the blessing as he recites it.

In modern times, the *tallit* is worn each day during the morning prayers (*Shacharit*), except on the Ninth of Av, when it is worn at the afternoon service, and on *Yom Kippur* (the Day of Atonement), when it is worn all day. The *tallit* is worn only during the day because the biblical commandment for its use specifies that the *tzitzit* must be *seen*.[5] In fact, the evening *Kol Nidrei* service on *Yom Kippur* begins before sunset, so that a Jew can wrap himself in his *tallit* while he can still see the *tzitziot*.[6]

Immediately after the recitation of the blessing, the *tallit* is put on, covering the head first. Then, the four corners are thrown over the left shoulder, a movement called *'atifat Yishme'elim* ("after the manner of the Ishmaelites, or Arabs").[7] After a short pause, the four corners are then allowed to fall back into their original position, two suspended on both sides of the worshipper.[8] Strictly observant Jews pray with the *tallit* covering their head, believing that to be enfolded by the *tallit* is to be enveloped by the holiness of the commandments of the Torah, denoting symbolic subjection to the divine will.[9] It is also customary in the morning service to press the *tzitzit* to the eyes and to kiss them three times during the recital of the final section of the *Shema* which deals with the commandment of the *tzitzit*. As a praying mantle, the *tallit* expresses and conduces to a spirit of sublime devotion and consecrated meditation, inspiring in the heart a feeling of awe and reverence.[10] A token of the honor which the *tallit* is accorded is seen in the fact that whenever Torah scrolls are moved, they are generally covered in a *tallit* to protect them.

The *tallit* stands on solid biblical ground as a means of drawing the Jewish worshipper to attention so that he remembers the commandments of God and enters with *kavanah* (intensity and devotion) into his time of prayer for passionate, intimate relationship with God. Bible-believing Christians would do well to respect this tradition and the piety of the Jewish people who observe it in honor of God.

Objects of honor of one faith should not be exploited and/or abused by those of another. Christians should be careful to honor the importance of the *tallit* tradition for the Jewish community by not misusing or co-opting the *tallit* for their own purposes. Some use these and other accouterments of Judaism to make themselves appear Jewish in order to gain some advantage in "witnessing" to Jewish people, thinking that somehow the end justifies the means. Such abuse and deception is unethical and should not even be considered, much less practiced among Christians. Others employ Jewish articles in an effort to inflate their own estimation of themselves as somehow being "Jewish." Wearing Jewish liturgical garments and displaying Jewish artifacts do not make one Jewish any more than donning a robe and a white wig makes one a British magistrate.

A growing number of Christians make such use of traditionally Jewish things in an effort to identify with the Jewish people and to demonstrate their understanding that their Christian faith is inherently Jewish. While such a desire for Christians to identify with the Jewish people is commendable, great care should be exercised not to misuse or misrepresent Jewish traditions. The Jewish people are certainly not impressed when a *tallit* is worn upside down, at the wrong time, or in the wrong manner. Christians who rush off to do Jewish things or to appear Jewish when they obviously know nothing of the subject are at best boorish and inconsiderate and at worst sacrilegious. We should remember that sensitivity is the Golden Rule in action.

Great lessons about the Jewishness of Jesus and the apostles can be learned from the articles which they most certainly used in their own worship of God. Every material article–like every spiritual exercise– which was patterned and modeled in the Hebrew Scriptures can be found in some way to point to the Messiah. This is both Jesus' and Paul's evaluation of the fundamental purpose of the Torah.[11] Truths that are profoundly enhancing to Christian faith are readily discernible in Judaism and Jewish practices. Metaphors and allegories can be legitimately drawn from these sources in the same manner in which the New Testament writers did; however, care should be exercised when doing so to ensure the fact that they are properly set in the context of the grammar and historico-cultural setting in which they were employed by the earliest church.

While Christians can certainly learn rich lessons about their Jewish Lord from the *tallit* tradition, they are not required to wear one when they pray. Indeed, the fulfillment of the command establishing *tzitzit* as a means of remembrance of God's commandments should be manifest in a fully biblical lifestyle of walking in the Holy Spirit and letting the light of God's Messiah shine through one's good works of obedience to God's Word. Christian believers who fully experience the living Christ are not merely enshrouded in the Torah, they are imbued with the living Torah through the indwelling lawgiver, the Holy Spirit.

It is unlikely that pious, Torah-observant Jews would begrudge Christians the legitimate, respectful use of any Jewish artifact that would draw a believer closer to God and his Word in pure, sincere devotion. If wearing a prayer shawl during times of prayer helps one to focus on and interact with the Divine, one could profit from such. If one is convicted by the Holy Spirit (not by one's own soulish impulses) that he should practice Jewish things, such an exercise is legitimate and is birthed in freedom, not in legalism. They are certainly of value correspondent to various material practices in Christian churches that are designed to focus the worshipper's attention on God and his service. If ministers wish to use a *tallit* as a vestment or if churches wish to use it as a parament in their sanctuaries at significant times to affirm their identity with the Jewish people, such use is appropriate. Objects like the *shofar*, the *menorah*, the *chanukiah*, the *tallit*, the *mezuzah*, the *matzah*, the *kiddush* cup, the Torah scroll, and others can add depth and richness to the Christian worship experience when they are identified with the living Christ.

A classic example of this depth that is added to the Christian experience by understanding the Hebraic matrix from which Christianity emerged is the subject of this book, the *tallit* tradition of Biblical, Second Temple, and Rabbinic Judaism. As we have seen, this tradition impacted the lives of prophets, kings, and ancestors of the Messiah in the Hebrew Scriptures and of Jesus, his disciples, and the people to whom they ministered in the New Covenant era. Without an understanding of this rich biblical tradition from the Judaic heritage of Christian faith, we have an incomplete view of what actually happened in Jesus' ministry. We are left to draw our own conclusions based on our cultures and traditions. With this background of the circumstances that were the context of events in the Gospels, we share a richness that expands our understanding and invigorates our faith. And, this is but one small element in the vast treasure house of riches that awaits those who search diligently to discover the Hebraic truths that often lie just beneath the surface of our Bible translations. Understanding the Hebrew foundations of our Christian faith is, indeed, a golden key that unlocks the treasures of Holy Scripture for those who passionately pursue the truths of God's living, infinite, immutable Word.

[1] Theodor Reik. *Pagan Rites in Judaism* (New York, Simon & Schuster, 1944), pp. 142-144.

[2] Martin Samuel Cohen. "The Tallit," *Conservative Judaism* 44 (Spring, 1992), p. 4.

[3] Rudolph Brasch, p. 240.

[4] Rudolph Brasch, p. 240.

[5] Alfred J. Kolatch, p. 101.

[6] Rudolph Brasch, pp. 238-239.

[7] Alfred J. Kolatch, p. 103.

[8] *Encyclopaedia Judaica* - CD-ROM Edition (Jerusalem: Judaica Multimedia, Ltd.).

[9] *Encyclopaedia Judaica.*

[10] Rudolph Brasch, p. 240.

[11] John 5:39; Colossians 2:17.

Epilogue: Living Emblems

It is not enough to be hearers and believers of the Word of God: we must be doers also.[1] For far too long, the Christian church has been characterized by dogmatic faith, championing belief but failing to practice what it preaches. It has focused on orthodoxy when God is more concerned with orthopraxy. Jesus affirmed that what would cause the church to be the light of the world would be its "good works,"[2] not just its faith or its doctrinal beliefs, be they ever so sublime. The world will immediately recognize his disciples, taking note of those who have "been with Jesus,"[3] when it sees the manifestation of transcendent love that is shed abroad in the believers' hearts by the Holy Spirit, a love that completely fulfills all the Torah (Law of God)[4] by imitating the life of Jesus in good works to "the least of his brethren."

We have clearly demonstrated the truth that is succinctly stated in Hebrews 4:12: "The word of God is alive and powerful." It is not a static, exhaustible resource. It is a living Word that brings renewal and fresh insight each time we examine it. By design, everything that is recorded in the pages of the Bible points us to faith in the Messiah. The panorama of events, characters, and material objects manifest by God among his chosen people were symbols, similes, metaphors, allegories, and types and shadows of events, characters, and spiritual matters that were to be manifest in the life of Christ and the church. The truth of this principle in no way diminishes the importance of what God did in pre-Christian times, nor does it minimize the value of what he continues to do with and among the his chosen Jewish people to this day. It does provide a foundation that validates the authenticity of what he has chosen to do among the Gentiles through the One who brought Israel's light to the nations.[5] Jesus is the new and living way who filled all the law and prophets full, adding depth and meaning to their predictive words by demonstrating what the Word made flesh would mean to the entire world: full and free salvation by grace through faith. He completed the faith of his Heavenly Father and of his earthly ancestors. validating its authenticity by providing an efficacious sacrifice that renewed and perfected the covenant and imbued it with eternal life.

The faith of what the church has almost pejoratively called the "Old Testament" is not some antiquated fossil religion that should long ago have been buried in the sands of time along with other failed systems. The People of the Book are not legalists who should have been assimilated into the nations where they were dispersed never to be remembered again. Both the people and the book are chosen of God and are manifestations of his immutability and of his irrevocable covenants.[6] God cannot lie, and he cannot change.[7] If Judaism were ever his system of religion for mankind, in some form it must remain so. And so it is. Biblical Judaism produced many Judaisms at the beginning of the Common Era; however, only two have survived, Rabbinic Judaism and Christianity, sister religions as it were. All that is authentic in religious experience today is that which is firmly rooted in the biblical Judaism through which Jesus and the apostles expressed their devotion to God.

The Word of God that the writer of Hebrews affirmed as "alive and powerful" was both the Hebrew Scriptures and the incarnate *Logos*. The "Old Testament" is the Bible that Jesus and the apostles used to preach the Gospel of the Kingdom. It is the "God-breathed" Scripture that is profitable for teaching and instruction in righteousness so that believers may be mature and equipped for every good work.[8] That is why it is so vital for the church to search the Scriptures, for what the Hebrew prophets, kings, and sages wrote as they were carried along by the Holy Spirit[9] is that which testifies of Jesus and Christian faith, validating both for all time as the fullest expression of devotion to God.

This is clearly true of the many material objects that God either designed himself or that his people constructed as manifestations of their obedience to his Word. They are, indeed, "living emblems," material symbols that take on life and meaning because of what they reveal. "The invisible things of [God] from the creation of the world are clearly seen, being understood by the things that are made . . . so that [men] are without excuse."[10] Just as the universe bears witness to the existence and nature of its Maker, leaving men with no excuse for failing to seek, find, and obey the eternal God, so the material objects that God instructed his people to fashion are semaphores that call man to remembrance. Ever pointing the way to God, these emblems stand as guideposts that escort him past the treacherous precipices of life into the safety of life-giving relationship with his Maker.

While our feeble attempts to fulfill the divine will do not always hit the mark and more often than not are imperfect and flawed, the attempt is what is important. Anyone who approaches God in simple faith will be "in no wise cast out."[11] When we seek to do his will, he accepts the best we have to offer and gently leads us toward the more perfect day. Visible symbols of faith and remembrance bring us to the more excellent way of pure and total love that is manifest both to God and to man, thereby totally fulfilling the requirements of all God's commandments.[12]

For the Jewish people, the *tallit*, the *mezuzah*, the *tefillin*, the *menorah*, and other objects that they have made in fulfillment of God's commandments to their forefathers are signposts along the road of faith that point the way in which they should walk (*halachah*). These objects are constant, visual reminders that they are God's chosen people and that their chosenness makes them servants to him and to the world. They are living emblems that bespeak the life and vitality of God's Word and his covenants with his people.

Christians, too, can profit from these living emblems, recognizing them as authentic expressions of devotion to God and his commandments and as objects that have fulfilled their avowed purpose in pointing the way to God and to interaction with him. For us, they point the way to Christ, expanding in their dynamic symbolism the meaning and depth of Christian faith, bringing richness and fulfillment to our lives. What God has said works!

This is especially true when we evaluate the richness of our heritage from the faith of Abraham manifest in the biblical Judaism of the Hebrew Scriptures. Both Paul and the writer of Hebrews instruct us that everything God commanded his people to do under the First Covenant adumbrated realities that were to be manifest in the New Covenant, giving us preview photographs as it were of the true and living Lord, the head of the church.[13] What Israel did and does literally in remembrance of God we must do spiritually. As we walk in the Spirit, the anointing that is in us by the gift of God's grace "teaches us all things,"[14] helping us in the process of *immatio Dei*, conforming us to the image of the living Christ.[15] As we walk with him in love, we discover the wonderful, affirming reality that "there is, therefore, no condemnation to them who are in Christ Jesus, who walk not after the flesh but after the Spirit."[16]

Rather than being an attraction to sideline us in routine, repetitious ritual, these material objects that God has inspired men to make from his written Word jog our memories and point us unfailingly to the living Word. We celebrate, not the objects themselves, but the Lord who is manifest in and through the principles that they reveal. The mature believer uses the object or symbol as a reminder, an aid to concentration on the invisible reality that the emblem represents.

We must remember that we are attuned to sensory perception that was created by God himself. We are impacted by what we see, what we hear, what we smell, what we touch, what we taste. Our faith, therefore, is not some sublime mental exercise or even an attempt to detach ourselves from both mind and body in some effort to contact the "god within" as monists do. Our faith is a living faith that involves every aspect of our being–body, soul, and spirit. We worship God with all our heart, soul, mind, and strength (body).[17] Even our meditation is a physical exercise in which we repeat over and over the very Word of God (the meaning of the Hebrew words for "meditate day and night."[18])

When we interact with God, therefore, it is not just through subliminal meditation. We see God, we hear God, we taste God, we smell God, we touch God—not literally, but through the things that he has commanded or that we have devised to literalize our interaction with him. We see God in visible symbols, We hear God in music and the spoken Word. We taste God in the Eucharist and in the table fellowship of the Christian meal that is shared with believers in any setting. We smell God in the rich aroma of the fruit of the vine, in the pungent anointing oil, in the incense, in the smoke of candles. We touch God when we hold his Word in our hands, when we embrace "the least of his brethren."

Emblems, then, are alive and powerful for us, for through them we materialize the Word of God, taking it from the abstraction of faith and manifesting it in the reality of good works that glorify our Father in heaven. Just as love is not love unless it proceeds from the abstraction of a substantive to the action of a verb, so faith is not faith until its germ seed is brought to full flower in good works.[19]

Emblems must never be ends in themselves. They must never become idols to which we direct devotion, nor must they ever be totems or talismans by which we hope to ward off evil. They must not be perceived as good luck charms. God has specifically commanded us that we are not to make "any graven image" or to "bow down thyself to them."[20] And they should not merely be artifacts or eye-pleasing objects for the interior decorator in all of us.

Emblems should ever be billboards that grab our attention in the maddening pace of the modern world, saying, "Stop!", "Remember thy Creator," "Make time for God," "Celebrate his goodness." We rush headlong, often down precipitous paths, striving to fulfill our ambitions, seeking for the satisfaction of self actualization. We need someone to ring the bell, flash the lights, and drop the barricade to keep us from being flattened by the "loco" motive that keeps us wrapped up so tightly in ourselves. God is that Someone, and the bells, lights, and barricades that he has erected are those symbols, emblems, and markers in time that he has specified in his Word.

For the Jew, the *tallit* is a daily reminder that he is to be enshrouded in the commandments of God, acknowledging his utter dependence upon God's grace and mercy. Every time he passes through the door of his home, kisses his hand, and touches the *mezuzah* that contains God's Word, he is reminded that El Shaddai is his protector. Each time he binds *tefillin* on his arm and on his forehead, he recognizes that God's commandments are to be written in his heart and in his mind.

What rich lessons these and other living emblems teach us as Christians! We have the *tallit* (uniform) of the Holy Spirit enshrouding us with God's Word. We have the blood of the Messiah applied to the doorposts of our hearts, and we have opened the doors of our hearts to his knock[21] and have hidden his Word within so that we might not sin against him.[22] The New Covenant has engraved his law on our hearts and in our minds by the *Shekhinah* of the Holy Spirit.[23]

And, because we have the living Christ within, we are well on our way toward being living emblems ourselves, living "epistles," written and read of all men, witnesses to the saving grace of God through the good news of the risen Saviour, to whom be praise in the church both now and forever. Amen.

[1] James 1:22.
[2] Matthew 5:16.
[3] Acts 4:13.
[4] Galatians 5:14.
[5] John 5:34-39.
[6] Malachi 3:6; Romans 11:29.
[7] Titus 1:2; Ecclesiastes 3:14, 15.
[8] 2 Timothy 3:16, 17.
[9] 2 Peter 1:21.
[10] Romans 1:20.
[11] John 6:37.
[12] Romans 8:4.
[13] Hebrews 10:1; Colossians 2:17.
[14] 1 John 2:20.
[15] Romans 8:29; 2 Corinthians 3:18.
[16] Romans 8:1.
[17] Mark 12:30.
[18] Psalm 1:2.
[19] James 2:20-26.
[20] Exodus 20:4, 5.
[21] Revelation 3:20.
[22] Psalm 119:11.
[23] Jeremiah 31:33.

Index

Restoration Foundation
P. O. Box 421218
Atlanta, GA 30342